Death Behind the Dunes
By
Sylvia Melvin

Evie,
I hope you enjoy
turning the pages.
Sincerely
Sylvia Melvin

© 2011 Sylvia Melvin
ISBN-13-9781463592080
ISBN-10-1463592086

Acknowledgements

Writing a suspense novel was a challenge I'd never considered until I realized while marketing my previous books that many readers enjoy that genre. Could I do it? For several months, scenarios played out in my head until finally my characters took on a life of their own. As a reader, I hope you enjoy the twists and turns that take you on a search for the murderer.

Like a farmer, I plant the seed in the form of words but in order to see an end product, others helped along the way. Many thanks to the following :

Major Steve Collier from the Santa Rosa Sheriff's Office took the time to answer my questions whether in person or by email. I appreciate how he kept me on an accurate procedural track.

Myra Shofner, my mentor and editor has the knack of motivation which keeps me moving forward.

Tommie Lyn Blackburn, a talented writer and computer guru patiently sees me through the formatting phase of publishing a book.

Al Melvin, my husband, whose eye for detail and photography, produced the cover.

The Panhandle Writers Group encouragement keeps me focused.

Thank you,

Sylvia Melvin

Chapter One

The throbbing ache behind Nick Melino's right eye intensified as he opened the front door to the glare of Florida's sun. When would he learn? It happened every time he savored the mellow taste of one too many Budweiser's. *Stubborn fool. Just like your father. It's true; ' the apple doesn't fall far from the tree'.* The memory of Janet's familiar words irritated him. What a nag! No wonder she was his ex-wife! Remembering her words, he needed to justify his behavior. He'd paid the consequences every time- like now. He'd had a good time last night. A twenty-fifth high school reunion is not your everyday social event. He hadn't seen some of those guys since the night they'd grabbed their diplomas and hit the road, scattering in all directions.

A smirk creased the edges of dark stubble that ran along Nick's firm jaw line. He was thinking how the years had done a number on many of his friends. The once taut, suntanned faces, with their trim, fit bodies, no longer resembled their owners. Instead, lines, etched from experience, ran across foreheads and crept around wiser eyes. Protruding stomachs and expanding hips showed a disdain for exercise.

Except for Lyndy McNeil-little change there. She stood out as she always had-confident, mature, physically fit and flawlessly beautiful. There wasn't a male on campus who wouldn't have sold his soul for a chance to date her. But only one guy savored that privilege. *And it wasn't me.* Nick sighed as he walked up to the paper box, extracted the folded mass of Sunday news, sports and coupons and tucked it under his arm.

"Hey, Nick," the bellowing voice rattled his foggy brain until he recognized it as his neighbor's. "Surprised to see you home today. Thought you'd be hot on the trail of that dead body, you being a detective."

"What are you talking about, Les? What dead body? Did I miss something in the past twelve hours?" Nick sauntered up to the property line.

Les looked Nick up and down. "Man you don't look so good. Tied one on last night, did you? No wonder you don't know what I'm talking about."

"A reunion out at Paradise Beach with my high school buddies. Worth every minute of this head-splitting hangover. So, who are you talking about? I'm supposed to know these things."

"She was at your party! Wearing a tee-shirt made up specially for your reunion. A couple of guys were plannin' on doing a little surf fishing and one of them tripped over her leg while he was toting his gear down to the water. Shot behind the dunes. Heard it on the news when I got up this mornin'.""

Adrenaline kicked in and knocked the grogginess out of Nick's head. His persona changed into Lieutenant Nick Melino, Detective at the Gulfview Sheriff's Office.

"What was her name?

Les pondered as he stroked his chin, straining to recall the news announcer's voice.

"Linda, no Lindsay or was it Lyndy?"

Nick's bloodshot eyes bore into Les's face. "It wasn't Lyndy McNeil! Tell me it wasn't!"

"That's it! Now I remember wondering when I heard it if she was kin to that wealthy family who own the boat building company on the south shore.

"Damn!" the word spat out of Nick's mouth like venom. His stomach churned and he fought the urge to throw up on Les's Sunday shoes. "Sorry, neighbor, but I've gotta go. Duty calls."

In seconds Nick was up the steps of his porch, charging through the front door muttering to himself, "There must be a mistake; it can't be. Not Lyndy! I need confirmation. Where's my cell phone?" Frantic glances around the living room centered on a small table beside his favorite La-z-y Boy chair. Only a TV guide lay on its surface. No phone. Impatience gained the upper hand as Nick feared the worst. "I'm losing it!" he said aloud. "I can't remember where I put my cell!"

"It's here," a familiar voice intruded, calming his panic. "On the cupboard by the fridge." A pixie-faced female walked from the kitchen toward him pushing layered strands of auburn hair out of her eyes. She stopped short. The expression on her face was not one of welcome. "Please, tell me you are not my father. You look awful and how many times have I heard Mom tell you that Budweiser makes you stink? Here, catch. I'm not coming one inch closer! And by the way, who was *your* designated driver last night?"

"Don't lecture me, Penny. I'm not in the mood. Not only do you look like your mother but you've inherited her ability to moralize too. So, maybe I took a small liberty last night. Case closed." Nick began to punch in the numbers at the Sheriff's Office.

"You should have called me; you're a cop. You put your reputation on the line. Do I have to wonder if you're drinking every time you're out of my sight?"

"Enough Penny, I...". Nick heard the dispatcher's voice and his tone became all business. "Marshall, this is Melino. Where's Andrews? Is he in this morning? Good. Connect me."

"Besides you were babysitting. No way you could have come to the beach for me," Nick shot back at Penny as he waited for his partner to pick up.

"Detective Andrews," came the response.

"Conner, Melino. Why wasn't I called?"

"Excuse me?"

"Last night –the dead woman on the beach. Was it Lyndy McNeil?" Nick held his breath.

"Yes, her mother identified the body about seven–twenty this morning. Seems her daughter was in town for a high school reunion."

Once again Nick felt a blow to his stomach and fought for composure. "You should have called me."

"Nick, it was my watch; and I knew you were out to party. Told me yourself you'd been waiting to cut loose ever since the divorce. Now be honest; what help would you've been on this scene? I'm surprised you're up this early. How'd you hear anyway?"

Truth dawned on Nick and he knew his partner was right. "Not important-neighbor heard it on the news. All precautions been taken to secure the scene?"

"You taught me well, Nick. It's under control. Take the rest of the day off and nurse that hangover. Oh, by the way," Andrews chuckled, "taking the 'hair of the dog that bit you' is just a wives' tale."

"I'm coming in, partner." Nick's voice trembled. "It's personal. Like every other red-blooded male in Gulfview High, I was in love with her."

#

September, 1986

The tackle came hard and fast. Eighteen year-old Nick Melino felt the full brunt of Brock Hamilton's body weight; and he cringed in pain as his legs went out from under him.

"Hey, Man, what's wrong with you? I'm on your team, remember?"

The star quarterback's eyes flashed with anger and he hissed at his team mate, "Keep your eyes on the ball, Melino and not on the good-looking blond over there. Lyndy's mine and I don't share!"

9

Nick staggered as he got to his feet and came face to face with his adversary.

"From what I've seen, you'd better get in line and take a number."

"Why you…" Brock's right arm came up and pushed Nick backwards against the approaching assistant coach.

"Okay, guys. Cool it!" He said as he stepped between the two players. "What's going on? This is supposed to be a practice or have you two forgotten we're playing the toughest team in the league Friday night. I saw that tackle, Brock. We don't need any injuries."

Brock's face reddened and his voice held a threat. "Coach Williams," he stared at Nick with eyes cold as steel, "You tell Melino to stay away from my girl and nobody will get hurt." He was gone before Coach could reply.

Garrett Williams looked at Nick. "So who's the girl? I'm the new guy around here?"

Nick's head motioned across the field to a group of cheerleaders going through their routine. A chorus of "P-A-R-T-Y, party, party is on this side. Hey, where's the party? The party's over here!" echoed in their ears.

"Lyndy McNeil. The one leading the squad. The girls voted her Captain last week."

Coach Williams scanned the group until he focused on a blond with shapely tanned legs and a smile that exposed perfect white teeth. "Hmm, I can see why your buddy's all worked up over that one. This may prove to be an interesting year," Williams chuckled. "I mean keeping the team focused on football."

Lyndy's eyes didn't miss the scrutinizing she got from Garrett and her curiosity grew.

"Hey, Alana, is that the new coach you told me about. Looks like he belongs in the movies - not on a high school football field. Good lookin' or what!"

"Get a grip, girlfriend, you need to read the school paper this week. There's an article on all the new staff. His name is Garrett Williams. He recently graduated from Florida State, won a bunch of athletic awards, and someday wants to go back and coach college football. And," she paused before continuing, " he's married."

Lyndy sighed. "I'm not surprised. Oh, well, just curious." As she picked up her gear, she changed the subject. "Oh, listen. Mom told me before I left this morning that Dillard's is having a sale on swim suits. Let's go. A girl can never have too many bikinis." As she stepped away from the sidelines, Lyndy brushed a strand of hair away from her right eye and glanced once more across the field.

Chapter Two

Pellets of hot water shot from the shower and grazed Nick's skin. He savored the aquatic massage, as energy replaced his earlier lethargy. As he guided a bar of soap over the muscles and fat that comprised his six-foot frame he sighed. *When did I start getting a paunch? Is middle age catching up to me? Time to start watching the diet. I definitely put away some liquid calories last night. Ahh, maybe all I need is another night of workouts at the gym.*

As Nick wiped the steam off the shaving mirror, a tanned, stubbled face with a firm jawline and blood-shot chocolate-brown eyes looked back at him. In less than five minutes, a few well positioned strokes of the razor took care of the whiskers. Any trickles of water left on his body evaporated with the swift movement of a thick towel.

After slapping a dose of Old Spice on his cheeks, Nick mused on his way to the clothes closet, *This ought to change my daughter's attitude toward her 'stinkin' father. When did she get so outspoken?*

A cursory glance at his wardrobe and his mind was made up. On any weekday he would have chosen a shirt and tie for work but today, even though he was going in, it was his day off. Jeans and a casual shirt was as professional as he intended to get.

Penny, still in her nightshirt with a slice of half-eaten toast in hand, met him at the bottom of the stairs.

"Wow! Now this is the father I hug every morning." She slung her arms around Nick's neck and squeezed tight. "Just give me twenty minutes and I'll be ready."

Nick stepped back and gave her a puzzled look.

"Dad! Don't tell me you forgot! We've planned this day together for two weeks." Penny's face fell and her eyes turned moist. " You promised to help me with my golf game. You told me my swing has a slice. I reserved a nine o'clock tee time at Liveoaks."

Nick held Penny's shoulders and looked into her distraught face. *Lord help me; I've disappointed her again.* "Baby, I'm so sorry; something has come up this morning. I'm on my way to the station right now. I swear if it wasn't personal I'd let someone else handle it."

"Why am I always last?" Tears ran through the freckles scattered above her cheekbones. "Last month it was my National Merit Award dinner. You missed it because of some shoot em' up druggie." Penny sniffed and rubbed the sleeve of her nightshirt across her nostrils. "Mom told me this would happen. No wonder she left!"

Nick dropped his hands and took a deep breath. " Don't go there, Honey - not now."

"What do you mean 'personal'?"

"A woman was found dead out at the beach last night. Someone from the reunion."

Penny gasped. "Who was she? How well did you know her? What happened?"

"She was a high school friend - just a friend - back during my teens." Nick's voice faltered as he listed Lyndy's attributes. "Head cheer leader, smart, full of spunk, a good looker to boot. The whole package. I owe her my best investigation. Right now I don't even know how she died."

Penny wiped her eyes and her voice softened, "Then give her your best, Dad. You're number one on the team."

Nick bent over his daughter and kissed her forehead. "I'll make it up to you, Sweetie. Hey, don't waste the tee time. Call that boyfriend who hangs around here. He isn't much of a golfer but he's a good guy." Nick winked at his daughter as he closed the front door behind him.

#

The moment Nick turned the key in the ignition of his car, the radio blasted forth with the tail-end of a song from the Golden Oldie era. Last night he was more than happy to sing along as he challenged the speed limit on his way home from the beach. Today, the beat of the music irritated his fragile nerves. He reached over to punch the off button. He paused.

The deejay's voice blared out. "Hey folks, that little disturbance out in the Gulf we've been tracking for the past few days is getting serious. Here's the latest from the National Weather Service. Hurricane Eileen, upgraded to a category four, is moving at thirty miles per hour and is expected to make landfall tonight somewhere between Destin and our turf - Gulfview. Evacuation is the order for those on the island and close to the water. Time to get out the hammers put up the plywood and get out of Dodge. Remember Ivan and Katrina."

"The last thing on my mind today is a hurricane, Buddy." Nick cut the deejay off with the flick of his wrist. *Guess I haven't been keepin' up with the news the past few days. Ahh, no big deal! This far inland...we'll be fine.*

Boarded up storefronts and long lines at the gas pumps reminded Nick that a certain wiser segment of the town's population was not brushing off the news but taking it seriously. He looked out the window at the sky that had been clear and blue just a couple hours ago. Bands of steel-gray clouds vied for position as they swirled overhead and crowded out the sun leaving the heavens looking ominous. The scent of rain hung in the air.

As Nick passed the local Winn Dixie, he noticed the parking lot was packed with vehicles.

Strange for a Sunday-Must be some kind of super sale. Then it dawned on him. *Of course! Storms draw people to the supermarkets like magnets. Survival - one of man's primal instincts. The pantries of Gulfview will be overflowing this evening. All in the name of 'hurricane supplies.'* Nick smirked. *These big chains love a good weather threat!*

So be it. The public was between a rock and a hard place; and that included him and Penny. Nick picked up his cell phone and called her. He couldn't remember the last time he'd actually shopped for groceries.

She picked up on the fourth ring.

"Yes, Dad. I hope this is important because I'm trying to put my contacts in and one of my lenses fell in the sink and it's probably down the drain!"

"Teach you to be so vain. You look great in those rimless glasses I paid over two-hundred bucks for just a few months ago. Whatever happened to them? Sorry, Baby. Don't run any water. You'll find it."

"Why are you calling?"

"Listen, there's a hurricane tracking our way and we'd better stock up on some supplies today. Be the sweet daughter you are and run down to the fridge and take a quick inventory so I can swing by the store on my way home."

A deep sigh of exasperation registered in Nick's ear and he could hear the clicking of his daughter's shoes on the tile floor as she entered the kitchen.

"Well," Penny commented, " I can tell you I ate the last slice of bread this morning and all I see in this fridge is a six-pack. You may think you can survive on alcohol but this chick needs a little more sustenance than that. Besides, I'm under age."

"Forget the sarcasm. Is there anything special you want?"

"Just the usual—milk, eggs, bread, juice. Probably should throw in some canned meat and veggies. You know the power's gonna go down -- always does. Oh, yeah, the peanut butter jar was empty when I looked this morning. I suppose we could survive on crackers and peanut butter. Truth is I'm getting kind of used to sparse vitals. One thing you can say for Mom, she knew how to cook and keep a pantry stocked."

Nick shook his head before he responded, "I'll take that as a hint that this father's talents in the kitchen leave a lot to be desired and his daughter is suffering from malnutrition. Yes, I agree with you. Your mother knows how to put a meal together. Apparently though," Nick's voice held a tease, "those skills were never passed on to her daughter. Love ya, anyway."

Before Penny had a chance to respond, Nick closed his cell phone.

Chapter Three

The drive from Nick's home to the Sheriff's Office normally took thirty minutes but since it was a main artery to the interstate, today, because of the impending storm, traffic was heavier than usual. Sedans, vans, diesel-powered one-ton trucks pulling R.V.'s , sports cars and motorcycles edged forward bumper to bumper and moved out of town at a snail's pace.

Last minute procrastinators! Should have stayed in their homes. Now they're sitting ducks. How far do they think they're gonna get before things turn nasty? That hurricane is forecast to track right up Interstate 65.

Each time Nick had to brake, his frustration grew. By the time he reached the turn-off for the office, he felt the initial stirrings of road-rage. As his Camaro came to an abrupt stop in his designated parking space, a gust of wind sent a spiral of dust dancing across his windshield. The fronds of several decorative palm trees in front of the main building swayed back and forth as though bowing to Nick as he ran for the front door.

Giving a cursory hello to the officer behind the glass-paneled reception desk, he took out his ID card and swiped it across the card reader beside the locked door that led to a collection of rooms. Offices, a finger-print cubicle, file storage areas and even a small kitchenette were seen only by staff. Folks who normally didn't work Sundays hurried past him darting here and there, preparing for the unknown. In advance of the approaching storm, computer cords lay coiled beside blackened monitor screens, hard drives were safely stored away and paperwork disappeared into folders that ended up in bulging file cabinets, while desk tops looked naked without the usual family photos. As he turned a corner on the way to his office, a couple of peers asked half-heartily, "Hey, Nick, thought you were off today. Or are you securing the hatches, too?"

With no desire to stop and chat, Nick tried not to appear rude. He nodded briefly, kept his pace and called back over his shoulder, "Checking on the death at the beach."

Nick reached in his pants pocket for a ring of keys, one of which would open the door to his office. Overhead lights immediately illuminated his twelve by twelve home- away- from- home. A plain mahogany desk, large enough to accommodate a phone, a computer setup, a vertical file holder, a jar full of pens and pencils and a can of beer nuts —one of his favorite snacks - took up a good portion of the room. A couple of straight-backed chairs sat to the right and a bookcase stood against the left wall with a photo of Penny on the top shelf. Vertical blinds, half-closed, covered a dust-streaked window pane. Plaques indicating promotion and certificates of Distinguished Service and Dedication hung in a haphazard formation around a wall-mounted clock.

With one hand, Nick swept a dried out doughnut into the wastebasket with a coffee-stained napkin and dialed Sergeant Andrews's number with the other.

"Conner, my office in five. Bring anything you've got on the beach case."

Before Nick had time to boot up his computer to check his email, a detective ten years his junior came into the office carrying a green file folder marked McNeil.

"Sorry if I was a bit flippant this morning, boss. Never guessed you actually knew the lady."

"Not as well as I'd like to have but that's water under the bridge. What do you have for me? We're working against time and Mother Nature on this one. Normally, I'd hand the reins over to you and let you run with it; but I know I'm going to eat and sleep every detail; so I might as well take the lead. Otherwise, I'll drive you crazy. You cool with that?"

"Cool, Nick."

"Okay. What do you have?"

Sergeant Andrews loosened his tie and opened a file folder and began to read. "2:01 a.m.: A 911 call to the Dispatch Center. 2:15 a.m.: Patrol Officer on scene. 2:27 a.m.: E.M.T. on scene, declares the victim dead. 2:43 a.m.: Death reported to Sheriff's Office."

He looked up from the report and continued, "I got the call from Major Roberts about three. I'd been watching a Sci-Fi movie on that late channel. Couldn't get to sleep last night for some reason. Think it was something I ate for dinner. Stay away from the China Doll, Nick."

Nick raised his eyebrows. "Andrews, the report! The report, please."

"Yeah." Andrews rubbed his stomach and grimaced. "Called Lewis and Meyers to meet me at the beach with flood lights."

"3:45 a.m.: Medical examiner arrived shortly after we did and immediately probed the victim's liver to check the temperature. She determined the victim had been dead for two hours and fifteen minutes." Andrews looked at Nick before continuing. "Still amazes me how that woman can be so accurate. Told us the victim's wounds and surrounding evidence indicated she'd been shot with a 380 automatic twice at close range. The patrol officer found one of the two casings three feet from the body. The second has yet to be found. Covered with sand no doubt. Hard to see something that small at night. Even with the lights."

Nick cringed at the thought of Lyndy taking her last breath as a bullet ripped through her chest. "Any sign of a struggle?"

"None. Dropped to the sand immediately. The examiner got plenty of blood specimens." Andrews checked his notes. "She moved the body to the morgue at five o'clock. I followed her to Sacred Heart and stayed while she made a preliminary I.D. By seven, the family received the news."

"Who took the photos?"

"I did. Why do you ask?"

"Because you're good at it." Nick gave a quick nod of approval. "And I want those pictures to be the best. When can I see them?"

"Been working on them for the past couple of hours. I took plenty; covered every angle, surrounding area, parking lot behind the dunes, the usual. Even a few spectators. You never know.

"So you're still processing them?"

Andrews nodded his head. "Yep."

"Keep at it. I'm going out to the island. I'm sure you guys did your job; but I won't be satisfied unless I see the scene for myself. Besides, daylight puts a whole new spin on things and the next few hours will be paramount. If you haven't heard, some dame by the name of Eileen is planning on paying us a call. And I don't think she's in a good mood."

Andrews sighed deeply, "Last thing we need is a hurricane messing up the scene. Sure hate to think of all that oil from the spill getting churned up and messin' up the beaches again. Course the experts tell us it's dissipated; but the locals know differently. Call if you need me. Right now I'm off to get another charge of caffeine. Hope the coffee pot's still plugged in with all the storm preparation going on around here this morning. These short nights are murder." He coughed, embarrassed by Nick's reproving eyes. "Excuse the pun."

#

Unlike the trip into the Sheriff's Office, the traffic was clear sailing out to the island - at least in the right lane. The left was a nightmare. An evacuation order was now in place and citizens were heeding the Emergency Management's Office's advice. Only the die-hard, stubborn ole geezers and some naive hurricane partiers remained with their in-your-face attitude and bottles of booze.

Heaven help them; because once this bridge is closed, they're on their own.

No matter how many times Nick crossed the bridge and came onto the island, he felt the lure of the environment. Its beauty spread out before him. How many times had one look at the ribbon of sterile white beach sand that ran along emerald green water enticed him to shed his shoes and go barefoot? His foot twitched as he recalled the feel of sand squishing between his toes. But, today, blood stained the pristine grains; and his heart ached.

Nick had no trouble locating the crime scene. The yellow tape that cordoned off the area had come loose from its moorings and flapped in the strengthening wind. Six patrol cars lined the side of the highway away from the parking lot, and a team of deputies were milling around. As he climbed out of his Camaro and shut the door, particles of snow-white sand the tourist brochures bragged about stung his cheeks like sleet in a winter storm. Wind gusts came, intermittently, swirling around him; and with each one, Nick's hopes of retrieving all remaining crucial evidence from the scene sank deeper and deeper into the sand. Mother Nature had her own agenda.

The sound of restless surf drew Nick's eyes toward the Gulf of Mexico where churning emerald green water, whipped into a frenzy, sent waves tumbling one after another onto the shore. Normally the usual Sunday crowd would be scattered about, soaking up the sun's rays, and shrieking with delight, as swimmers splashed and dived into the aquatic playground. Today, Nick's trained eyes saw not a soul sauntering along the lonely stretch of sugar-white sand. He sighed, relieved.

Don't need any spectators getting in the way. Got enough to deal with by the looks of it.

One of the patrol officers caught sight of him and shouted, "Over here, Sir. The body was found behind this dune."

Nick acknowledged the officer with a nod. "Mornin' all. Tough searching through all this sand, isn't it?"

"Sure is Lieutenant." replied another officer. "Now I know what they mean when they say it's like looking for a needle in a haystack." The other officer, the short one, laughed.

"Meyers," Nick beckoned to another detective to join him. "Need to talk to you."

A man in his thirties, with trim physique, and fatigue written all over his face tread carefully through the sand up to the dune.

"Looking for this?" He pulled his notebook out from a pocket in his sports jacket, produced a folded sheet of paper and handed it to Nick.

"You've been out here all night, eh?" said Nick as he scanned the paper. Pretty detailed diagram. Now show me all the particulars. Oh, and just for the record, I have a personal stake in this case. This time I'm the lead agent but I'm going to need everyone's expertise."

"No problem, Lieutenant." Myers moved closer to Nick and put his finger on the diagram. "As you can see, she was found lying on her back. Her head slightly tilted to the left, the right arm bent at the elbow with palm up, fingers slightly curled. Left arm extended horizontally.

Knees drawn up toward her stomach and pointed to the left."

"Where was the gun?" Nick's voice faltered.

"Looks like the impact knocked her off balance and it slipped out of her hand and landed about six inches from her hip."

"Personal items?"

"A woman's small denim purse. Cell phone, driver's license, keys, credit card, hair brush, lipstick-the usual women's stash. No note, if that's what you're thinking. Oh, a flashlight was lying in the sand, too. Andrews took everything back to the Office. I'll go over it again when I'm through here."

Nick slapped Meyers on the back. "Good work but you're finished for now. I can see you're tired. Now, go home and get a few hours rest. I don't want you missing anything because of fatigue."

Meyers gave Nick a half-hearted grin, started toward his car, and then stopped, turned and said, "The personal part. You knew her, didn't you? Sorry 'bout that."

Nicked shrugged. "Yeah, it's a long story."

#

As the team scrutinized every cordoned - off square foot of sand and parking lot, highly agitated sea gulls shrieked their disapproval overhead, jostled about by gusting winds, and none too appreciative of Nick's men intruding on their territory. Sea oats arched and whipped about, as visibly disturbed, hyperactive sand crabs scurried over the beach, as if searching for the entrances to their sanctuaries down below.

By two o'clock, the only other relevant evidence found near the body was the missing shell casing. Besides that, nothing but a few discarded soda cans, a reel of fishing line, a child's plastic shovel and a bottle of Coppertone rewarded the team in their search for clues. As the tide grew higher and the winds blew stronger, sporadic raindrops intensified; and their heavy plops indicated there was more to come - a lot more. Turning towards his car, Nick did one last quick survey of the site, knowing full well that by this time tomorrow, if the forecasters were on target, he wouldn't recognize this place.

Giving his best wolf whistle, he got the team's attention and motioned to the patrolmen at the far end of the barricade to gather round.

"Just got word from headquarters that the bridge is being closed in about twenty minutes. We've done our best here; nothing else has shown up, so pack up guys and head back to town. I expect most of you have family you need to attend to. Be careful. See you back on duty tomorrow. Good Lord willing."

Nick lingered as each patrol car left the scene. Hesitant to leave, his eyes drifted back to the dune where Lyndy took her last breath. Shifting sands erased the imprint of her trim body. *Thank God I didn't see her stretched out lifeless and bloody. It's the woman with the dancing eyes, unruly blond curls, and lilting laughter I want to remember.*

Two questions remained unanswered. *Suicide? Maybe. Murder? Possible.*

Chapter Four

The change was apparent the moment Nick walked through the front door of the Sheriff's Office. Gone was the hyped energy felt earlier when folks were scurrying around preparing for the storm. Missing were the voices bantering back and forth about damage predictions. No two-way radios squawked. The reception area phones lay silent. Only the rhythm of fingers making a soft repetitive click on a computer keyboard broke the eerie silence as a skeleton crew went about their business waiting for the big event.

The sound of the security door buzzer echoed down the hall as Nick swiped his key card across the scanner.

A rookie officer sat alone at a desk in a cubicle studying a robbery report.

"Hey, Tom, didn't you recently become a new father?"

A smile lit up Tom's face. "Ten days ago. A boy, eight pounds four ounces. Named him after his grandfather-Luke Haines."

"Your first?"

Tom nodded. "Our first. Told my wife we can't let him grow up alone. Needs a little sister."

Nick chuckled, "Probably wasn't the best time to suggest another child, eh?"

"You're right. Says I can have the next one; and it would be okay with her, if I spent more time at the office."

Nick gave Tom a good-natured slap on the back. "She'll get over it. But let me tell you something." His tone became serious. "Today he's a baby. Tomorrow he's a teenager. Spend time with Luke. Don't let this job rob you of something you'll never get back."

"Yes, Sir."

"That's who you need to be with tonight. Whatever you're doing can wait 'til tomorrow. I'm covering for you. Now get out of here."

Tom expelled a deep sigh. "Lieutenant, I can't thank you enough. I'm having trouble keeping my mind on my work knowing Eileen is about to hit and my wife and baby are alone. Deeply grateful, Sir."

He gathered some paperwork together and stuffed it into a folder. "Oh," he said, "Dominoes came by and left us a bunch of free pizzas. Guess the last thing on anyone's mind today is ordering pizza so they had to do something with the leftovers. If you're hungry go for it."

The smell of pepperoni and cheese reminded Nick that it had been almost twenty-four hours since he'd eaten. As he bit into the first slice, he suddenly remembered the grocery list he'd compiled in his mind and knew without a shadow of a doubt that by the time he'd leave work, Winn Dixie employees would have vacated the store.

Dang. Penny is home alone with little to eat. I've let her down again.

Nick reached for his cell phone and dialed his sister. She picked up on the second ring.

"Sis, listen, I've been at work all day and it looks like I'm here for awhile longer. Could Penny come spend the night with you? I don't want her alone with a hurricane ready to break loose and there's nothing in the fridge to eat. As usual, my good intentions didn't work out." Nick paused and politely listened to a minor scolding from his older sibling.

"Yes, I know, I have to get used to being Mr. Mom, too. These past few months have been hectic and stocking the pantry wasn't real high on my priority list. I owe you one, Peg. I'll call her right now and tell her to hike on down to your place. Talking me into buying a house on your block was brilliant." Nick chuckled, "Even though you made a mint on the commission. Love ya. Bye."

Nick dialed his home number and Penny answered immediately. When she didn't put up an argument about spending the night with her aunt, Nick knew she was also apprehensive about the storm.

"Dad," she paused a second before continuing, "Mom called. She's concerned and wanted to know if we'd be better off leaving town. Said we could come to Jacksonville."

"Hmm, showing her sweet side, is she?"

"Actually, it didn't last long when I told her you were at work on your day off. Another tirade you probably don't want to hear. So I assume the invitation is refused."

"Truth is Penny, I'll hunker down here, at least until the worst is over. Got a ton of work to do on this beach case. Lots of questions and at this point there are few plausible answers."

"You'll solve it, Dad. You always do. Just be careful, okay? Love you."

"You too, Baby. Oh, tell me, how did the golf pro do?"

"We didn't play. They closed the course because of the weather. But, I got a free pass for another time."

"Keep your date book open, Honey. I promise you we'll work on that swing."

#

Knowing how important it is in an investigation to interview family, friends and witnesses before the memory starts receding and playing tricks, Nick picked up his phone with a heavy hand and dialed the McNeil residence. By the fourth ring, Nick was hoping it wouldn't go to an answering machine, a male voice said, "McNeil residence. Martin speaking."

The face of Lyndy's older brother, a candidate running for a Florida Senate seat, flashed before Nick's eyes.

"Lieutenant Mileno. I'm lead agent on your sister's case. My sincere sympathy to you and your family." Martin offered no response. "Lyndy was a friend in high school. In fact, our crowd spent many hours on your family's tennis court."

"Melino? Nick Melino?"

"You remember me?"

"Saw your picture in the class year book two nights ago. Lyndy had it out to take to the reunion." Martin's voice was cold.

"I know this is difficult but I need to talk to the family."

Martin cleared his throat before answering. "The doctor has sedated Mother so she's unavailable today and of course it's anyone's guess what the hurricane is going to do. Since my sister took her life..."

Nick stopped him in mid sentence. "That determination has not been made. We've just started the investigation."

"But we were told a gun was by her side. Smells like suicide to me. Shouldn't take you long to wrap this one up, Lieutenant."

Nick's neck grew warm and his breathing quickened. He sensed he was being manipulated. *Rule number one— keep control of the investigation.*

"I'll check with you again tomorrow. Your cell number please. In the event the phones are out of order."

By the time Nick finished with Martin McNeil, a sterile chill ran like a shock through his body. What kind of man would show such a lack of any sense of loss over the death of his sister?

#

The promised stack of photos sat on Nick's desk. As much as he wanted to delve into them and look at the evidence, something kept holding him back. First he made a trip to the men's room, then decided he was thirsty and went for a coffee only to find the cold contents of a half-filled carafe. He searched his pockets for change and selected a Coke from the soda machine. On his way back to his office, he peered out a large picture window someone had reinforced with tape. The rain no longer came down in buckets, but swept across the parking lot in blinding sheets of storm-driven torrent. Overhead lights flickered in the building giving warning of impending darkness.

Settled once more, Nick put his emotions aside and opened the folder. He stared at a woman he barely recognized. Wind-blown, shoulder-length blond hair covered half of her face, her body lay as though she were sleeping, her hands clenched. The hardest part to look at was the wound itself. Blood saturated her reunion shirt covering most of the letters that spelled Gulfview High across her chest. Tears welled up in Nick's eyes and ran freely down his cheeks.

Why, Lyndy? Why? Suicide or murder? I promise you I'll find the answer.

Chapter Five

By seven-thirty, the power was out and a generator kicked in to supply limited power to the Office. Outside, the rain continued and the wind screeched upwards of eighty miles per hour. Nick groaned and wondered if Penny had managed to collect the table umbrella, lounge chairs, pool paraphernalia and anything else that could become a wind-blown projectile. He imagined his 'Gator' chair landing in the middle of Les's prize rose garden. *Sure hope it doesn't hurt my chair. Oh, well, I guess that's why I pay hurricane insurance. If she didn't, it's my fault. Should've reminded her earlier.*

Nick fought fatigue as he arranged the photos on the tile floor as close to Meyer's diagram of the scene as best he could. When he finished, it looked like a giant puzzle, each piece visually telling a story but silently challenging Nick to find the untold truth. The old cliché about a picture being worth a thousand words ran through his mind and Nick was grateful he had a partner who played by the rulebook: "Always take photos from the outside in;

general to specific. Important evidence may be on the perimeter."

Thank goodness computers have come a long way to enhance images since I started thirty years ago. These shots are so good I can feel the sand.

Suddenly, Nick became aware that the only sound he heard now was the purr of the generator - no rain, no wind, no thunder. All was calm. He got up from his position on the floor and pulled back the blinds. Light from a full moon bounced off the water in the flooded parking lot. As he stared in wonder at the power and beauty of nature, he realized what was happening. Eileen's eye, well defined, was passing overhead but he knew this respite would be short-lived. The south-west quadrant of the hurricane was still to come - normally not as brutal as the northeast quadrant; but nevertheless, it could deliver a violent punch.

Turning back to the photos, Nick picked up one of Lyndy's car. It was no surprise to see that she drove a Lexus. *It suited her; money and style were always her trademarks. Apparently, the advertising agency she founded was quite successful. And then she was her 'daddy's little girl' so an inheritance from his death a couple years ago probably set her up for life.*

Funny how she never remarried after she and Brock broke up. Guess marrying your high school sweetheart, even if he was the star quarterback, doesn't always work out.

Nick closed his eyes and let his thoughts wander back to the reunion. The reception room at the Shifting Sands Hotel transported him back to his youth where a huge banner hung above the double doors displaying the school's mascot, a smiling dolphin, that welcomed the Class of '86.

"Come get a name card and sign in, Nick," called Alana, one of the few faces he recognized in the crowd. "Be sure and put down your email address and phone number. Never know who might want to keep in touch. Course you and I bump into each other every now and again around town, don't we?" Nick smiled in agreement and before he could respond, Alana continued, "Not like so many of our peers who high-tailed it out of Gulfview to gosh knows where."

Nick put down the pen and asked, "Did Lyndy make it home?"

"Sure did. Just look for the blond with most of the guys fallin' all over her. Nothing's changed in that department. Some women have all the luck."

"You didn't do so bad yourself, Alana. Mike's a hard worker, isn't he? That seafood business is a real asset to our community. The best shrimp in the Gulf."

"Until the oil spill. But I don't want to go there - not tonight. Tonight's a night for fun; so mosey on over to the bar and get yourself a drink, my friend."

"The best advice I've had all day. Think I'll do that."

Nick leaned against the bar and slowly let the cold, frothy liquid trickle down his throat. His eyes raked the room until he spotted Lyndy, the real reason he decided to show up at this affair. Nick watched as wispy blond tendrils bounced around the high cheekbones of her flawless oval face each time she moved her head. *Gorgeous! Time has treated her well.*

Butterflies fluttered in his hardened cop's stomach. "Excuse me; excuse me," he repeated while he navigated around several bodies of various shapes. Finally, he stood before her. Their eyes met; and in an instant Nick felt like a teenager again.

The smell of Lyndy's perfume and the softness of her cheek as she flung her arms around his neck and hugged him sent his pulse racing.

"Nick Melino. Look at you. Still as handsome as ever. And to think you're a detective." A voice as smooth as silk teased at his ear. "Now does that mean I have to behave tonight?" She released her hold on him and laughed.

"I left the cuffs at home. Great to see you, Lyndy. It's been awhile."

"Hey," Lyndy slipped her arm through Nick's and said, "it's getting too crowded for conversation in here. Let's head out to the patio. We can sit around the fire-pit and catch up on our lives."

"Super. Let me grab another Bud. What can I get for you?"

"Perrier and lime, please. I've turned over a new leaf."

"Probably a good move. My daughter thinks I drink too much. She may be right but in my line of work something has to dull the senses. The things I see are not easily forgotten. So far, it hasn't interfered with my job. I'm still at the top of my game."

Nick guided Lyndy to a couple of lounge chairs far enough from the fire to be comfortable, but close enough to enjoy the flickering flames.

"I don't see a wedding band; but, you mentioned a daughter." Lyndy looked puzzled. "Divorced, widowed?"

"Divorced almost a year now. Penny lives with me. Didn't want to move to Jacksonville with her mom."

"Can't say I blame her. Gulfview still has a small town atmosphere. There're times Altanta can be overwhelming. Traffic everywhere!"

Nick used his art of questioning to dig further. "You never remarried after you and Brock split?"

For a second, Nick saw sadness sweep across her face; but it quickly changed to a soft smile. "No, my passion is, Heather, my daughter. She's my life. We're very close. For the past two months she's been doing research in Europe for her doctorate in art appreciation. You know, visiting all the galleries and the old masters."

"Think you'll ever move back?"

"Doubt it. Of course, Mom's not getting any younger; but she still rules the roost and insists I live my own life. I come back for all the holidays; and of course, I wouldn't have missed this for the world. It was Alana's idea, you know. We keep in touch constantly. Couldn't live without email. "Girl talk," Lyndy giggled. " Some things never change, Nick."

"How long will you be staying?"

Before Lyndy responded, a boisterous male staggered toward them waving his hand, as his drink sloshed over the edges of his glass. "Hey, Lyndy, Coach Williams is here. How 'bout rounding up some of the squad and giving him a cheer; for old times sake?"

Lyndy shook her head. " Nah, this body ain't what it used to be. Besides I'm not sure I remember those cheers."

"Oh, c'mon, girlfriend," Alana, chimed in, as she appeared with a couple other members of the'86 squad. "Just for laughs. We couldn't keep you quiet in the ole days."

Lyndy took Alana's insistence as a challenge and stood up. "All right. Round up MaryAnn and Shirley, too. We'll need all the help we can get."

The background music of Billy Joel faded into the distance and the MC for the night asked the crowd to quiet down as the girls got into position. Nick sauntered over to Coach Williams and shook his hand, "Congratulations on Friday night's win. Thought the Rams had us on the ropes; but as usual; you had a trick up your sleeve. Took me back a few years to a game or two we played."

The lines crossing Garrett William's forehead and the graying hair at his temples did nothing to diminish his rugged athletic appearance. A big smile welcomed his former student. "Nick, good to see you. Hey, the team of 86 won the championship. You guys taught this rookie a lot."

Nick lowered his voice and bent close to Coach's ear. "There's a rumor going around town that one of Florida's best high school coaches is in the running for a position in Tallahassee. Is it true?"

"Melino," Coach feigned shock, " the detective in you never stops, does it? I'd be a proud to have that feather in my cap, but no comment." Eager to change the subject, he turned and looked in Lyndy's direction. "The captain of the cheerleaders still looks like the prom queen I remember. Lyndy McNeil. Some students you never forget."

As if on cue, Lyndy stepped to the microphone and directed a lingering gaze on Coach Williams. Her soft, mellow voice rippled through the room. "This one's for you, Coach."

The years seemed to dissipate as six women flung their arms high, kicked their legs up in unison, and delivered a personal, spirited patriotic cheer:

"Coach told the team to hold the ball high,
We were the best, do or die!
Rah! Rah! Rah!"

The room exploded into applause, laughter and enthusiastic shouts. Coach Williams walked over to the squad and hugged each one to show his appreciation. Nick noted that the embrace Williams reserved for Lyndy lingered a little longer than the rest and didn't miss that his hand slid down her arm and squeezed her fingers.

Hmm. Thought Nick. *Stop it, Melino; you're letting your fantasies get the better of you.*

The night wore on and the noise level rose as Nick strolled about the reunion, with a drink in hand, renewing old friendships, and reminiscing about times past. By midnight, he knew his blood alcohol level was dangerously high and decided to put an end to his revelry. Working his way to the door, he caught sight of Lyndy coming out of the ladies room.

"Leaving so soon, Nick? And we haven't danced yet."

"Afraid my co-ordination leaves much to be desired after a few rounds of brew. Stepping on a lady's toe isn't considered kosher for a southern gentleman, my dear. So let me give you a hug and leave you unscathed."

Lyndy welcomed his embrace and added, "It's been wonderful seeing you again, Nick. We were such good friends. I've never forgotten you. You were the best lab partner a girl could ever want. Always covered my mistakes."

Nick stepped back but continued to hold her hands. His eyes looked deeply into hers and he said, "You don't know how many times I wished I could have walked in Brock's shoes."

A coy smile parted Lyndy's lips. "You never told me that."

"Because your heart belonged to someone else." Nick squeezed her fingers before saying, "Call me the next time you're in town."

"I promise. Drive carefully. Stay safe."

The last words he heard Lyndy speak still rang in his ears.

#

Nick's vision blurred from strain; and as Hurricane Eileen roared back to life, he walked over to the lounge and claimed an empty couch. He didn't expect to sleep well, but before the next round of thunder and drenching rain returned his snoring matched anything heard outside.

Chattering voices and a ray of bright sunshine brought Nick out of his slumber.

For a second, he felt disoriented and his first thought was of Penny. Was she okay? Could he reach her? And what was all this noise?

"Hey, Melino, pulling some overtime?" The sheriff 's booming voice brought a round of laughter from those waiting for the coffee to finish dripping. "The night shift's already gone. Looks like you ought to join 'em."

Nick wiped his eyes and stretched to get the kinks out of his cramped limbs. "Say Sheriff, how' bout we pass the hat for a full size bed for us dedicated guys. That couch just doesn't cut it."

"What do you think we're running here, ole timer, a rest home?" A twinkle in his boss's eye put a smile on Nick's face.

He was almost out the break room door when Sheriff Kimbal walked over and stopped him. He lowered his voice.

"Heard you knew the McNeil woman, Nick. I know your intensity when it comes to solving a case. Keep things in perspective; and don't wear yourself to a frazzle. I need you. Penny needs you. And one last thing," Kimbal paused and his eyes met Nick's, "Alcohol never solved one case."

Before Nick could respond, Kimbal patted Nick on the back and concluded, "Just a rumor- just a rumor."

"And a false one at that," muttered Nick as he made his way to his office. "So what if I stop in for a beer a couple times a week with a few of the guys. It's never interfered with my work. Relaxes me; makes me think better. When did my drinking habits become a problem around here?"

"Who you talking to, Nick? Has this case sent you over the edge or somethin'?" asked Andrews as he stepped up his pace and followed his partner down the hall and into his office.

"Careful. Don't step on the photos," warned Nick. " Nice job. One of your best. Start checking out those tire prints. Want the make and model of every vehicle that is factory-equipped with these."

"Been over the Lexus grill to bumper; she kept a clean car. Nothing there." Andrews quipped, folding his arms across his chest and watching Nick studying a photo of some footprints. "Somethin' is bothering you about this whole situation, isn't it? You're thinking she was followed, aren't you?"

"Anything's possible, Conner. You've been an investigator long enough to know that."

Andrews nodded his head in agreement.

"So change of subject. What kind of damage did Eileen do last night?"

"Oh, she had a temper tantrum alright, especially in the north eastern end of the county. Heard there was a tornado that played havoc with a couple barns up on 87. Lots of pine trees snapped off and we'll be seeing FEMA start bringing in the blue tarps for roofs. Enough damage to start the insurance companies whining again. They'll be lobbying for higher rates, wait and see. Power's still out in certain parts of town, mine included; but the utility trucks are out in force this morning. My place went pretty much unscathed, except for oak limbs and garbage all over my yard. Can't believe that ole gal who lives three doors down left her garbage container out all night. Hard to say what county it landed in."

Nick smiled and stroked his itching chin whiskers as he thought for a moment.

"Well, here's a tentative plan for the day. I'm going home to shower. Then, I hope we can drive over to Cypress Point and interview the McNeil family. I talked to big brother yesterday and I sensed some attitude there."

"Martin McNeil? The one running for the Senate? Got his face plastered on every billboard in town?"

"That's him. I get the impression he likes to be in control." The muscles in Nick's jaw tightened. "Not this time, Martin!"

#

Nick glanced at his watch on his way out the door and decided to take a chance that his sister's household might be awake. Peggy answered on the third ring; her voice groggy with sleep.

"Sorry, Sis, had to know if the roof's still in tact on your house; or, will you be looking at a blue one for the next few months."

"All safe and secure, little brother. We had a few hairy moments I don't care to repeat. Penny didn't sleep much so she's dead to the world right now. You get any sleep?"

"Curled up on a too narrow sofa and felt like a pretzel this morning but I'll survive. I'm on my way home to a cold shower before I go out to the McNeils and see what I can find out about their daughter's death."

"She's the one that had you dancin' on a string, wasn't she?"

"Me and the rest of the team."

"Didn't she marry Brock Hamilton?"

"Yep-short lived though. Divorced after a couple years."

"Sad," Peggy's voice grew quieter, "death is always so sad." After a moment's silence she perked up and made an offer her brother couldn't refuse. "Drop by and have breakfast with us after you freshen up. Penny told me a mouse couldn't find enough to eat in your house. As soon as the power comes on, we're going shopping to take care of that situation. How does grits, and bacon and eggs cooked on the grill sound?"

"I can smell it already."

As Nick turned onto his street, the sound of chain saws and generators broke the early morning solitude. Tree branches hung askew and threatened to topple below to the leaf-covered lawns. Missing shingles left barren spots on several roofs.

A nagging sense of anxiety turned to relief as Nick drove into his driveway and saw that the lone pine tree between his property and Les's had snapped in half and lay a mere two feet from his garage.

How many times have I said to myself, 'Next time there's a hurricane that pine's comin' down. Need to take care of it soon before it's too late.'

Nick wiped the sweat from his forehead and a spontaneous prayer of thanks fell from his lips. He knew he should be joining his neighbors in the cleanup; but right now something more important was on his mind. He had a case to solve.

Chapter Six

"So what kind of mood is Martin McNeil in today, partner?" Andrews slipped on a pair of sun shades and turned the ignition key of the patrol car.

"Told me he hoped we wouldn't keep him long. Needs to get down to the community center to help organize a relief station."

"Real compassionate sort isn't he. Rackin' up votes if you ask me. Pandering to the public's sympathy. Sister's not even buried yet and he's out looking after the welfare of his fellow citizens. What a trooper! Trouble is, there's too many folks out there who'll buy it."

"Guess it's safe to say," Nick shot a smirk at Andrews, "candidate McNeil won't be getting your vote!"

"C'mon, Melino, it's nothing more than a photo op. He'll be on the six o'clock news tonight passing out bottles of water."

"By the looks of some of these residents cleaning up their property, they just may need him." Nick gave his partner a gentle jab to his right shoulder. "Think I'll hire that teenager down the street to help clean up my yard. Penny says he's bad news; but, maybe some honest work will keep him out of trouble for a while."

"Just lock up the house while you're gone. And maybe you ought to lock up your daughter, too."

Nick shook his head. "Not Penny's type. She's a pretty straight- laced gal. I know it's hard to fathom considering the genes her father passed on." Nick's voice grew serious, " Can't believe she's off to college next year. I'm hoping she'll stick to Northwest Florida and forget about applying to one of those distant Seminole or Gator campuses."

"And what have you got against the two best schools in Florida? One of which happens to be my Alma Mater."

"Nothing. It's just that after too many years and a failed marriage, I'm finally getting to know my daughter. She could have gone with her mother but since this is her senior year, she wanted to stick it out at Gulfview and graduate with her friends. After my reunion this weekend, I understand that now more than ever." Nick looked away.

Ten minutes later, Andrews pulled into a tree-lined driveway marked 'Private'. As the car approached the house, his eyes grew bigger at the sight of a two-story home that looked as though it belonged on a plantation during the Civil War. The red brick exterior contrasted with two circular white columns that supported an upper balcony. Wicker furniture lined the wrap-around porch and a huge oak door, flanked by stained glass graced the main entry.

"Wow! What I wouldn't give for a pad like this!" Connor almost ran off the driveway gawking at the

McNeil residence. So this is what's meant by 'old money'."

"Wait 'til you see the back," Nick volunteered. "Pool, tennis court, manicured gardens. There's a fountain big enough that you could almost swim in it."

"So how'd you get so familiar with the place?"

"Football team had an open invitation to Lyndy's parties."

"Lucky you," Andrews replied as he pulled up behind a Mercedes. The initials MM on the license plate left no doubt who owned it.

Before the two men had time to climb the porch steps, the front door opened and a tall brunette rushed into Nick's arms.

"Alana," said Nick, "surprised to see you here."

"Oh, Nick, isn't it terrible? I was probably the last person she talked to at the reunion. We were the last to leave. I gave her a big hug and she got in her car and drove off." Nick stepped back and looked into eyes brimming with tears.

"She was the last one I hugged, too. Great to talk to her. Caught up on each other's lives. We drifted apart after she moved to Atlanta, you know."

The stricken woman wiped her eyes, sniffled, turned to Andrews and extended her right hand. "I'm sorry. Where are my manners? I'm Alana. Lyndy was my best friend. We were inseparable. Remember Nick? Everyone around school called us the 'Terrible Two's'.

Nick smiled and started to introduce his partner when Andrews accepted her welcoming hand and cut in, "Conner Andrews. Sorry about your loss. It hurts to lose a friend." His hand lingered in Alana's until he saw Nick's raised eyebrow.

Nick returned to his original question. "Why are you here, Alana?"

"Miss Katherine needs me. I practically grew up in this house. My mother was Robert's...er, Mr. McNeil's personal assistant. From the time I was a little girl, I came home from school almost every day with Lyndy. I even went on vacation with the whole family a few times."

"So you know the McNeil's pretty well?" questioned Andrews.

"I should say so," Alana said as she opened the door and ushered the men into the marble - floored entry. "C'mon into the study; Martin and Miss Katherine are waiting for you."

A white-haired matronly lady rose from a wing-backed chair and walked toward the detectives. Dressed in a simple black sheath dress, matching pumps and a single string of pearls, she welcomed her guests with a genteel southern drawl.

"Gentlemen, please come in and find a comfortable seat. I'm Katherine, Lyndy's mother and," motioning toward her son, "this is Martin, Lyndy's brother." Martin offered no handshake but nodded in return. His mother continued, "Terribly hot isn't it. I apologize but since the power's out, we're only able to run the generator and air conditioner for short periods of time." Katherine looked at Alana. "Dear, bring some lemonade. It may not be cold; but it will quench our thirst."

"Ma'am," Nick took the lead. "I'm Lieutenant Melino and this is Sergeant Andrews. We offer our sincerest sympathy. I graduated with Lyndy."

50

Katherine gave Nick a long look. "I thought you looked familiar. You're the one who taught her how to play tennis."

Nick smiled. "Your daughter could give that ball a wallop. I remember many a game when she whipped me good."

Martin shuffled from one foot to the other and finally spoke up. "Lieutenant, could we get to the point of this meeting and stop going down memory lane? As I told you on the phone, I'm expected at the Community Center."

"Now you don't have to be rude, Martin," scolded Katherine, her voice registering all the authority of a true matriarch. " Lieutenant Melino was always welcome in this home. In fact," she said, turning to Nick, " I never could understand why Lyndy didn't pick you for her sweetheart."

Nick felt warmth exploding into color around his neck and it wasn't caused from the hot weather. *Time to move on.* He looked at both and asked, "Do either of you know a reason Lyndy would have taken her life? Let me ask you about some areas of her life that may have been troubling her- relationships, finances, health issues, depression?"

At that moment, Alana walked into the study carrying a silver tray with the lemonade Katherine requested, and proceeded to pass out the refreshment.

Martin cleared his throat and made a confession. " Gentlemen, my little sister was the apple of my father's eye. That was no secret. He granted her every wish. She was spoiled rotten!"

"Martin!" Katherine's mouth opened in shock. "How can you talk about your sister like that and her dead less than forty-eight hours? Have you no shame?"

"You know it's true, Mother. She always had to be the center of attention. She was a rebel, too. My guess is she took this charade too far."

Andrews jumped into the conversation and asked, "Is there anyone who might have wanted to harm Lyndy?"

"What are you suggesting, Sergeant? Murder? She hasn't lived in Gulfview for twenty-five years for heaven's sake. Or, were you thinking of someone close to home?" Nick saw the sneer on Martin's face as his cell phone rang and he quickly left the room. In seconds he was back and announced that he needed to leave. Before he departed he turned to his mother and asked, "Do I need to call our attorney to sit in on this inquiry?"

Nick spoke first. "That won't be necessary, ma'am. No one in this house is under suspicion."

Katherine took a deep breath, squared her shoulders and stated, "Martin, you are excused. We'll talk later. Alana, I would like to speak to these gentlemen privately. Close the door on your way out, please."

The room was heavy with anticipation. Only the ticking of a grandfather clock penetrated the silence. Andrews and Melino looked at each other waiting. Finally, Katherine, dabbing her eyes with a cotton handkerchief, her voice trembling spoke.

"Gentlemen, my daughter did not commit suicide; she was murdered and I can prove it."

Nick looked at this wounded woman and wondered. *Is it denial?* How many times had he seen a family member, especially a mother, reject the idea that one of their own could take away the life she had given them?

"How, Mrs. McNeil?"

"The necklace was missing. When I went to the morgue to identify her body, the necklace was not around her neck. It was given to her by Robert, her father, the night of graduation. It was very valuable; twenty-four carat gold and had been his grandmother's."

Andrews inquired, "Did you ask the medical examiner if she was wearing the necklace when Lyndy was brought to the morgue?"

"I did. No jewelry was found on her body."

"Did you check her bedroom and suitcase? Are you sure she wore it Saturday night?" asked Nick.

"I saw it with my own eyes. In fact, I joked with her as she fixed her hair that an antique piece of jewelry and a fifteen dollar tee-shirt was an odd combination. She just laughed and said it was her good luck charm." Katherine lowered her voice to a whisper, "Not this time."

Nick pulled the photo file out of his briefcase. He secured a couple shots of Lyndy's body from the pile and studied them for a moment before passing them to his partner.

Andrews confirmed what the photos revealed.

"I took these photos, Mrs. McNeil, and you're correct. I saw no necklace on her body. "

Tears ran down Katherine's cheeks as she tried to put relief into words. "I knew she wouldn't take her life. Not my baby. I don't think I could live with suicide. Murder is bad enough."

Nick reached over and patted her hand. "Mrs. McNeil, you understand we'll have to prove it was murder. Until we do, the assumption is that it was suicide. Because of the gun."

Katherine held onto Nick's hand and for the first time he saw a glint of light in her eyes as she said, "You'll prove it Nick Melino. I know you will-for my girl."

Chapter Seven

The click of two seatbelts and the rush of static from the two-way radio were the only sounds heard in the patrol car as it departed the McNeil residence. Neither Andrews nor Melino spoke. From the intense expressions on their faces, each knew the other was silently mulling over the conversations with Katherine and Martin. Half-way to town, Andrews blurted out, "It could've been murder; I've got a feeling that ole gal is onto something. She doesn't miss a trick. Did you notice how she put Martin in his place?"

Nick stroked his chin and nodded. "He's a hot-head, alright. Seems pretty convinced Lyndy was going to use attempted suicide as a grab for attention. For the life of me, I can't imagine why she'd ever think she needed to resort to a stunt like that. My guess is that big brother wants this supposed suicide all tied up and filed under "Case Closed" as soon as possible."

A smirk parted Andrews' lips. "Ah-ha, a murder investigation is not the kind of publicity a candidate wants before an election. I see where you're comin' from."

Nick nodded his head in agreement.

"The missing necklace bothers me, partner. Now that I think of it, she was wearing that necklace; because as we talked by the fire, the glint of the flames on its facets caught my eye. I don't suppose the medical examiner has been able to complete her work yet; but, if it was forcefully taken off Lyndy's neck the metal may have left marks in her skin." Nick gave a deep sigh. "These power outages can sure put a crimp in things."

"So you agree we may be looking at murder?"

"Don't be surprised if the name on the file reads 'Homicide'."

To Nick's surprise, the lone pine tree that had lain beside his garage when he left was cut up and piled in a neat row along the wall. Pine cones, sawdust and broken branches still littered the driveway. A familiar face, flushed and dripping with sweat looked up and motioned for Nick to stop.

"Les, what are you doing cleaning up my mess? Man, you don't have to do that. In fact, I'm on my way in to change clothes and get busy."

"No big deal, Nick; just returning a favor."

Nick's brows furrowed. "What did I do for you? You don't owe me anything. Except maybe a beer when I bet you the Gators would take Tennessee last Saturday. But I'll forgive you, friend."

"I'm talking about that speeding ticket I got. Appreciate you talking to somebody; the damage could have been a lot worse. Not to mention the nights I would have spent in the dog house. The little woman wasn't near as mad as I thought she'd be." A roll of fat jiggled over the top of Les's shorts as he chuckled at his folly.

"Just keep that lead foot of yours off the gas pedal, okay? I want to keep my job. And I can't do that running interference for you!"

Nick felt uneasy groping around in his dark bedroom in the shadows looking for a pair of clean shorts and tee-shirt. *Oh, well, with any luck the power will be on soon. Being on the same electrical grid as the hospital has advantages.*

On his way out the door, he had a thought. *A beer would sure go down good before starting to drag all the debris over to the curb. Les definitely deserves one for all his hard work.*

One Budweiser turned into two before he realized an hour had passed with little to show for his clean-up efforts. To make matters worse, Penny came riding down the street on her aunt's bike.

"So this is how a hard working detective spends his day. Sitting around getting sloshed while his neighbor does the work."

"For your information, little lady, I've had a very productive afternoon. Needed the nourishment to finish the job Les started. Give me a break. In another hour or so, you'll never know Eileen came to call."

Penny shifted her weight on the bike and prepared to cycle back up the street. She was halfway down the driveway when she stopped and turned her head in her father's direction and announced, "Dinner's at five-thirty; Aunt Peg says don't be late. Oh, I almost forgot. Gramps will be there, too."

Guilt washed over Nick and he tried to remember the last time he had spent any quality time with his father. *A month, maybe two at the most. I know we went flounder fishing in the bay. 'Bonding time' the younger generation call it.* An old unpleasant memory surfaced as Nick dug his rake into the pine sawdust. But it was not enough to distract himself from something he'd rather forget.

Frank Melino used fishing at night as an excuse to bury his sorrow in a bottle he kept hidden under the bow of the boat. As the hours passed, the more intoxicated he became, until he maneuvered the aluminum John boat on a course that became more and more erratic.

"It was my fault, son. I sent your brother to die that summer night. You were just a wee thing. I should have gone to the Tom Thumb myself but your mother was at a meeting and you were asleep."

"Dad, don't torture yourself. I know the story."

Frank took another swig from his bottle and ignored Nick's request. "We needed milk for breakfast and the store was only a block away. The robber gunned him down without a second thought. Cold blood. A twelve year-old boy."

The tears streaming down his dad's face left Nick's gut wrenching. No matter how much he tried he couldn't alleviate his father's pain.

Frank looked off into the distance and for several minutes neither man spoke. Finally, broken, he looked at his son and muttered, "You ready to go in?"

The rising sun signaled the end of the floundering. Nick knew his father would go home and sleep off his stupor-until the next time.

Alcohol wasn't the answer. Nick knew that. But, if he admitted it, he'd numbed his own senses more than once. Reality can be a hard cross to bear.

Haunting questions still lingered in Nick's mind about his younger brother's death. *Do I push harder, dig deeper and go the second mile to avenge my brother's murder? Will Dad ever come to terms with this? And did this cost me my marriage?*

By five-o'clock the pile of debris waiting for the city's clean-up truck reached its pinnacle and both men declared, "Job completed." A quick, cold shower and a clean change of clothes transformed Nick into a man on a mission again. This time it was one of his sister's home cooked meals that captured his attention. He couldn't wait to feel the warmth of family after all of the events of the past week-end. It'd been rough and tomorrow didn't look like it was going to be any better. Tomorrow he'd attend Lyndy McNeil's funeral.

Chapter Eight

The parking lot of Hope Presbyterian Church looked like a used car lot. Vehicles of every color and model occupied the spaces until the overflow parked on the side of the highway. It didn't surprise Nick that a huge crowd turned out to pay their respect to Lyndy and her family. Seaworthy Boats was an old established company in Gulfview and many a family depended on it for their bread and butter.

Before leaving his car, Nick called Andrews for a last minute briefing.

"Conner, you and Myers split up. I want one of you in the back of the church watching the entrances and exits and one in the balcony getting an overall view of the congregation. I'll be up front; I want to see who comes near the casket. Follow the hearse to the cemetery after the service and spread out again. One of you hang around after the family leaves and make small talk with the guys who fill in the grave. See if they know anything that might be helpful to us."

Nick paused and listened to Andrews for a second then continued, "That's what I'm thinking. It wouldn't be the first time the killer hung back to be sure the victim was gone. Talk to you later."

The smell of dozens of colorfully designed floral arrangements overwhelmed Nick's nostrils the moment he stepped into the sanctuary. They formed a semi-circle around an exquisite rosewood, satin-lined coffin. As custom in the south dictated, the family stood near their loved one and greeted the line of mourners. Nick fell in behind a group that hugged, cried and lingered longer than necessary. He didn't mind the wait as it gave him time to observe the surroundings. Lyndy's mother showed stalwart reserve while Martin made sure he shook every hand as though he were conducting a political rally. Beside Mrs. McNeil stood a young woman that took Nick's breath away. For a moment, he had to remind himself that Lyndy was dead. The resemblance to his friend, the body in the coffin, left no doubt in his mind that this beautiful creature had to be Lyndy's daughter.

Eventually the line edged forward and Nick offered his hand to Martin. A limp response was followed by a hushed statement. "I don't appreciate the way you're handling this, Lieutenant. Mother doesn't need to be grasping at straws by chasing dead-end theories."

Startled, Nick returned, "This isn't the place or the time, Martin. I'll talk to you later."

He moved on to Mrs. McNeil who in pretense of a hug, whispered into his ear, "Do you have any news? Call me." Immediately, she reached for the young lady beside her. "Lieutenant, this is my granddaughter, Heather. She arrived yesterday. The storm held her up but thank the Lord she's here now."

Nick took Heather's extended hand and asked, "How was Europe?"

Surprise registered on her lovely face. "How did you know I was abroad?"

"Your mother and I were friends and we chatted at the reunion Saturday night."

Heather's eyes glistened with fresh tears and she said, "So you're one of the last persons she talked to before…" The sentence hung in the air.

Nick nodded. "Yes."

The shuffling of impatient feet gave Nick a hint that he needed to move on. He squeezed Katherine McNeil's hand and assured her he'd keep in touch and then made his way to the sanctuary for the service.

Soothing organ music set a reverent mood as mourners took their seats and waited for the service to begin. Nick saw nothing that aroused suspicion among those that came up to the coffin. Once the family took their designated pew, the pastor commenced to speak.

As he read words of comfort from scripture, Nick noted familiar faces from the reunion. Coach Williams sat with an anguished, tight-lipped expression on his face, his eyes fixed on the coffin. Alana dabbed her mascara-laden eyes with one hand while she draped the other arm around Heather's shaking shoulders. Eulogies expressed by friends reminded everyone of Lyndy's zest for life and how much she'd be missed. After thirty minutes, the pallbearers wheeled her body out a side door and the congregation walked to the front entrance and scattered throughout the parking lot.

Nick met up with Andrews and Meyers; and they decided to ride together in Nick's Camaro to the cemetery.

"Think we ought to keep a low profile out here; don't want to scare anyone off by showing up in a patrol car."

"Big funeral," observed Meyers. "Lots of folks paid their respects."

"Did either of you see any suspicious behavior," asked Nick.

"Not from where I was sitting." Andrews said, glancing over at Meyers. "How 'bout you?"

Meyers shook his head. "Nah, not a soul got up and left."

"Mingle out here among the folks and watch for stragglers or anyone else who sticks out from the rest of this crowd."

The graveside service was short. Less than half of those who attended the church came to the burial site. Before long, just the men with the shovels remained. A tear gathered in Nick's eye and he took one last look at the gaping hole in the ground then turned and walked away.

I can't stay and listen as they cover you up, friend.

Back in the car, Andrews commented, "We may have chased a rabbit today but at least we covered our bases. Maybe it was suicide, Nick."

Nick was quick to come back. "Don't forget the missing necklace; I'm not closing this case 'til I see the examiner's report and satisfy myself about what had to have happened."

\#

By Wednesday the power was back up and life showed signs of returning to normal around Gulfview. A call to the medical examiner confirmed that her report would be faxed within an hour. Nick paced the floor of his office. Every ten minutes he glanced at the clock. His instincts told him he was onto something but he needed confirmation from another source.

As Nick circled his desk for the sixth time, Andrews came rushing through the door waving a newspaper high in the air.

"I knew the guy was hiding something. I knew it!" He slammed the paper down on Nick's desk and pointed to the local headlines-McNeil Holds 'em and Folds 'em.

"What are you talking about, Conner?"

"Martin McNeil has a gambling problem. Apparently, his opponent's been doing his homework and has dug up some dirt. Read the article."

Nick reached for the paper, "Doesn't surprise me. These politicians play hardball."

As his eyes worked their way across the printed page, his interest deepened and by the end of the article he commented, "Hmm, seen in Biloxi several times at the Poker and Black Jack tables. No wonder he's pushing for casinos in Florida. The big boys in the industry may be putting the squeeze on him."

Andrew's face was beaming. "And to think we didn't have to lift a finger."

"Slow down Conner, nobody's said he did anything illegal but if Lyndy's examination shows what I think it's going to, I'll be paying Martin another call."

As if on cue, the fax machine rang and the swishing sound of the paper being fed and printed captured both men's attention. Nick grabbed the report as soon as it stopped printing. For years now, he'd read dozens of these reports but never as thoroughly as he scrutinized this one. When he read the line, 'lacerations found around victim's neck' he let out a victorious, "Yes! Lyndy's vindicated. It's not suicide. Mark her folder homicide, Conner. And roll up your sleeves, we've got some work to do!"

Chapter Nine

"Yes, Lieutenant, ten o'clock will be fine," confirmed Katherine McNeil. "Martin, of course, is down at his campaign headquarters and Heather left five minutes ago to fly back to Atlanta. There are so many loose ends to tie up in these situations, you know. See you shortly."

In less than thirty minutes, Nick and Conner stood before the massive oak door and listened as the doorbell chimed throughout the McNeil's foyer. Katherine, looking weary after the events of the past few days, ushered them in with a wane smile.

"We'll meet in the living room gentlemen. It tends to be dark in the study and I need some sunshine in my life today."

Nick spoke first. "Well, we may have brought you a small ray of that, Ma'am." He seated himself on a brightly patterned sofa and opened a file marked McNeil-Coroner Report. "I'd like to read to you exactly what the medical report states."

Katherine sat beside him with baited breath.

"Lacerations and abrasions found around the victim's neck with attendant bleeding consistent with a necklace or other object being forcefully removed." Katherine gasped as her hand caressed her own neck.

"Murder! Lieutenant! Didn't I tell you it could never be suicide? But who hated my beautiful baby so much?" Tears glistened in this wounded mother's questioning eyes.

Andrews answered, "That's our job to find out, Ma'am."

Nick returned the report to the file folder and took out a notepad. He cleared his throat and proceeded with caution. So far Katherine's co-operation had been positive. He didn't want to risk turning the tables by insinuating her son was a loser and might know something about Lyndy's death.

"Mrs. McNeil, there was an article in the paper yesterday that suggested Martin may have gambling debt."

Before Nick continued, she cut in. "Politics is a nasty business. It seems now-a-days you can say anything you want about your opponent and get away with it. Didn't used to be that way; civility has gone by the wayside. To be honest, I saw the headlines but couldn't bear to read another blot against this family. When you get my age, there's only so much bad news you can take."

Both men nodded in agreement and replied, "Yes, Ma'am."

A moment of silence followed and Katherine confessed, "But I can't hide the truth. When Martin graduated from college, Robert offered him a position in the company. Trained him from the beginning. He was a fast learner and more and more responsibility fell on his shoulders since my husband wanted to step down as president." Katherine paused, took a deep breath and continued, "Martin had access to all the records of Seaworthy Boat's business transactions. He was, I believe it's called "cooking the books" and skimming company profits to pay off gambling debts. When Robert realized what was happening, he was furious. Keep in mind my husband was a Scotsman and their thriftiness is legendary. Thievery was not tolerated in this house - even by his own son."

Andrews and Melino took notes as Katherine continued. "When the will was read after Robert's death two years ago, Martin received a pittance and Lyndy got her share as well as her brother's."

Nick's expression revealed to Katherine what he was thinking. She nodded her head and closed her eyes. "I pray he didn't have anything to do with her murder, Lieutenant. I know my heart couldn't stand it."

Nick patted Katherine's hand and tried to console her. "Don't jump to any conclusions at this stage of the game, Mrs. McNeil. As Sergeant Andrews told you, it's our job to find Lyndy's killer and we have a lot of ground to cover yet."

By the time Nick returned to the office after lunch, two calls from Martin McNeil were on his machine and he suspected the ringing phone would make a third. Before the machine kicked in Nick answered, "Lieutenant Melino …"

A familiar voice cut him off. "Melino, I told you I don't like the way you're handling my sister's death. How dare you lead my mother to believe she was murdered.

Stay off our property or I'll have you in court for harassment."

Nick fought to keep a professional tone. "Mr. McNeil, the medical examiner's report states in no uncertain terms that there are lacerations and abrasions on Lyndy's neck. A valuable necklace is missing - one that I personally saw her wearing two hours before her death, heavy enough and of a design that would have left such wounds. Reason enough to suspect foul play."

"Circumstantial evidence, Melino. Never hold up in court. Keep away from us you hear?"

"Martin, let me give you a piece of valuable advice. Stay close to town and don't give another thought to complicating my investigation. There's a little matter of some gambling debts I'd like to discuss with you. And by the way, where were you Saturday evening at one fifteen?"

"None of your business, Melino! We're done talking to each other!"

All it took was one smart-mouthed remark from Martin McNeil to rev up Nick's gears. To hear, especially from his mother, that Lyndy's brother was skimming money off the top of the boat building business to cover gambling debts came as a surprise. It was criminal activity alright; but, if he was never charged, there was probably nothing the law could do about that now.

Sounds like his father dished out appropriate punishment the old fashioned way. Just hope for Katherine's sake Lyndy didn't catch the brunt of Martin's anger.

Nick buzzed Andrew's extension. "Conner, what's the name of that convenience store out on the island down from the parking lot?" He paused for an answer. "In and

70

Out, that's it. Wonder if they're back up and running yet? Think I'll give them a call. Most of them use video surveillance. I'll run out there and see if they have a recording of events for last Saturday night. Have you or Meyers started working on getting those vehicle tire prints identified?" He paused again. "I know the storm set us back a day or two but it wouldn't surprise me if a Mercedes is one of them." Another pause. "You're right pal. He may be our man."

Chapter 10

Three things in life excited Martin McNeil. Money, power, and expensive toys. He grew up in a privileged home where wealth and prestige were synonymous with the family name. His father, Robert, earned his fortune by physically working with his hands at the boat yard and transforming his knowledge into a successful business career.

Martin showed no inclination to do either. He favored a fast buck and the casinos in Mississippi soon became a regular haunt. Sometimes he'd drive over to gamble. Other times, he'd fly his dad's plane over to Biloxi, especially if he really wanted to impress someone. His IOU's at the gaming tables increased enough to warrant continuous paranoid glances over his shoulder. He could never be sure when his benefactors would lose their patience with him and start calling in markers. Desperate for funds, the temptation at Seaworthy Boats to skim money off the profits bit at his heels like a persistent puppy. At first, no one was suspicious since he managed the books and with his degree in accounting and business, he knew how to help himself without attracting unwanted scrutiny. The Bahamas had offered a safe haven for his deposits until the day his father brought in an expert to audit the company accounts. The careless error of a few misplaced figures pointed a finger of guilt at Martin.

Rather than fire his son, Robert used an old school tactic - humiliating demotion.

Not a civil word passed between them for the next two years and not a tear was shed on Martin's part at his father's death. The shock of being disinherited surprised him and gnawed at his barren heart. Anger replaced any love he had for Lyndy every time he thought of her getting his share of the fortune. Now, he counted on the last ace in his hand.

I've got to win the senate seat. Florida's ripe for casinos and if I can get a bill passed to make gambling legal my debts will be forgiven. The backroom boys have as much as told me so.

Martin picked up his cell and dialed his campaign manager. "Ben, do whatever it takes to keep Detective Melino away from me and this center. The last thing I need is a murder investigation involving the McNeil name spread across every media in Florida. My sister's death was suicide. Plain and simple. Got that?" Martin waited for a response. "Good, now make sure that T.V. ad we worked on gets plenty of air time. That little bit of dirt you dug up on my opponent might be the ammunition I need to win this thing."

#

Now that the emphasis on the McNeil case was on homicide instead of suicide, Nick knew his days and night could get crazy. He hated it when he and Penny passed like the old cliché said, 'ships in the night.' Since Sunday the most time he'd spent with her was five hours. *Have to do better than that. Maybe she'll ride out to the beach with me this afternoon. Yeah. That sounds good. I'll even up the ante a bit.*

Satisfied with his decision, he flipped his cell phone open and called his daughter.

"Yes, Dad. I'm doing my pilates."

"Sweetie, I have to drive out to the beach this afternoon on business; interested in spending some time with your absentee father. Dinner at the Half-Shell?"

"My favorite restaurant!"

"Anything I want on the menu?"

"You name it."

"Give me time to shower. See ya."

On the drive to the island, Nick got an update on the courses Penny needed to take to complete her diploma, activities and sports she was involved in and the latest gossip around the campus. It felt good to talk about things positive; since his world dealt so much with the negative.

Every so often Nick stole a sideways glance at his daughter. "You know you look the image of your mother. Some say you have my eyes but believe me your profile is a dead ringer for her."

"I'm taking that as a compliment, Dad. She's hot stuff!"

"Always was, Honey. So is she dating anyone? Just curious."

Penny gave Nick a teasing smile. "Or a tiny bit jealous? A guy she works with took both of us out to

75

dinner the last time I was visiting. Nice fellow - boring but nice. But then what can you expect from an accountant?"

"Not dashing like your father who lives a life of excitement and daring seven days a week!" joked Nick.

"I think mom would have settled for less excitement and more of you." Penny's tone reeked of accusation.

"It's in my blood; a drive that's difficult to explain. I can't change. We both came to terms with it. She left. You know, Penny, I believe once you've loved someone, truly loved them it doesn't matter what direction your lives go in, you carry a piece of that person in your heart. I'll always love your mother."

"And what about that woman at your reunion who died? Did she have a piece of your heart, too?"

"Yes. In fact, that's why we're out here. She didn't kill herself; some important evidence shows someone else did. I'm hoping to pick up a surveillance tape at the local convenience store. Anyone who came in or out will be on the Saturday night tape. This one's too important for me to miss anything."

"I'm sorry you lost a friend, Dad. I remember in ninth grade how sad we all felt when one of the boys on our soccer team got run over by a truck."

Nick reached over, squeezed Penny's shoulder and changed the subject. "Hey! Enough sad talk. How 'bout a run on the beach before dinner?"

"You're wearing a suit and tie for heaven's sake."

"Won't be for long. Here's the store. Let me do my job and then it's off with the tie and on with the shorts. They're in my gym bag - been there a month. I'll change in the men's room."

Penny held her nose and made an ugly face. "Phew! They'll probably have to fumigate the place!

In fifteen minutes, Nick returned to the car wearing a pair of Nike shorts, a suit over his arm and his leather shoes stuffed into a gym bag.

Penny was quick to note he didn't have a video tape. "So where's the tape?"

"Struck out. The owner's gone and the kid behind the counter is not authorized to relinquish any surveillance videos."

"Bummer! Not even to the police?"

"I could get a court order but it's too late today. I'll be back."

Penny gave him the thumbs up sign. "That's my dad; once he's hot on the trail of a killer, he never gives up."

"This trail's just starting to heat up, Honey. Whoever the guilty party is ain't seen nothin' yet."

Chapter Eleven

Nick did his best to balance a hot cup of coffee in one hand while he fumbled with a set of keys trying to find the one that opened his office door. The ringing telephone sounded more like an impatient baby crying , "Stop everything! I want your attention. Now!"

Nick made a dive for the receiver, spilling coffee down his tie. *Great. This is not a good omen. I need every ounce of caffeine I can get this morning. This better be good.*

A surly faced Lieutenant put the phone to his ear. "Melino here."

"Good mornin', Lieutenant," each drawn out syllable oozed with southern charm. "This is Heather, Lyndy's daughter. We met at the funeral."

Suddenly, coffee didn't matter any more and Nick's attitude made a complete turn-around. "Of course, what can I do for you?"

"Grandmother told me the evidence warranted a change from suspected suicide to homicide. Is that true?"

"Yes. I'm expanding the investigation."

Nick heard the relief in her voice. "Thank you for keeping this case alive. You could have stamped it suicide and gone about your business."

"I could never have done that to your mother, Heather. But I have to be truthful; so far we haven't anything concrete."

Heather's voice became hushed and Nick strained to hear her say, "I need to talk to you in private. I'm back in town. I'd invite you here but Uncle Martin had a fit when I mentioned your name last night. Said you're not welcome in this house ever again. Can't imagine why he's so convinced it was suicide."

Nick's body temperature shot up and his breathing became shallow. But, he hid his anger. "Come into the office today. The décor's not too great but the coffee's pretty good. When can I expect you?"

"About eleven. One of Grandmother's friends is taking her out to lunch so I'll be free. I hope what I'm going to disclose won't shock you but it may have a bearing on Mom's case."

Nick's curiosity peeked but he knew better than to ask too much too soon. He simply said, "See you later."

Despite the fact that five other homicide cases needed Nick's attention, the McNeil case kept rising to the top of his list of priorities. What started out as a routine investigation began to expand. For the life of him, Nick couldn't imagine what shocking information Heather was ready to divulge that would have anything to do with her mother's murder.

The next four hours lagged; and his level of irritation increased like an itch he longed to scratch, but couldn't reach. He entertained the idea of driving to the In and

80

Out to try to get his hands on that security tape but a call to the convenience store revealed to him that the owner was out of town on a family emergency. The tape was locked in a safe.

Exasperated, Nick walked to the lounge, and emptied the dregs left in the coffee maker into the garbage and then proceeded to make a fresh pot.

Can't serve the lady stale coffee after bragging so much about it.

Mission completed, he checked to be sure the supply of Styrofoam cups wasn't depleted. It wasn't. No fancy china mugs sat in the cupboard but it was the best he could do.

Nick glanced at his watch - two more hours. Maybe Andrews had something on the tire prints. Two doors down from his office, Conner motioned for his partner to join him.

"Just got off the phone with Tom's Tires. You know that guy can tell the make and model of anything that's on the road from any print I give him. Man he's good!"

Nick's interest heightened and he leaned toward Conner.

"So what are we looking for?"

Andrews read the list.

"Dodge Ram, a Ford mini van, a Chevy Malibu and a Galant," he said, glancing at Nick with a look of distain. "Why can't folks in this country buy American?"

Nick ignored his question and asked, "Is that it?"

"Of course, the Ford Ranger the two guys who found Lyndy drove. And this all assumes that the subject vehicles are still equipped with the original tires provided by the manufacturer."

"No BMW?"

"Not according to the photos I showed Tom."

Disappointment subdued Nick's enthusiasm. "I was hoping to make an unexpected visit to Martin McNeil's headquarters. And I wasn't intending to make a campaign contribution."

"Still doesn't let him off the hook, Nick. He's got motive; we just need some other hard evidence."

Nick nodded his head in agreement. "Speaking of leads, I got a call from Lyndy's daughter this morning. You remember her from the funeral."

Andrews gave a soft whistle. "Hard to forget that one. Now I understand why you were so attracted to her mom in high school. What's on her mind? I thought her grandmother told us she'd gone back to Atlanta."

"She's back in town. Says she wants to talk to me. Thinks she has some information that we need to know but her uncle forbids us to step foot on their property."

Andrews sarcasm put a smile on Nick's lips. "You just gotta love the guy, don't ya?"

"She'll be here shortly so put your jacket back on and straighten your tie 'cause I want you as witness to this conversation. Besides," Nick winked at Conner, " you're a Braves fan, aren't you? Never know what that could lead to."

Promptly at eleven o'clock, a deputy escorted Heather to Nick's office. Immediately, both Nick and Conner got to their feet and Nick extended a welcoming hand.

"Good to see you Heather. This is Conner Andrews, my partner on this case."

Heather turned and gave Conner a melting smile as he lingered over the handshake.

82

"It's so reassuring to know that competent men are handling my mother's case. Grandmother can't say enough good things about you, Lieutenant."

A flush of warmth surged through Nick's body and he felt embarrassed by the blush he knew reddened his cheeks.

"We're giving it all we've got -- which isn't a whole lot to be honest, Heather."

Nick looked at Conner and suggested, "Why don't you run down to the lounge and bring us back some coffee. Fresh pot. Made it myself."

Conner looked into eyes the color of the sky on a cloudless day, and asked, "Sugar and cream?"

Her gaze met his, "Sugar, please. One teaspoon." The silken threads of her speech connecting one syllable to another mesmerized him until Nick jolted his friend back to reality.

"Conner. The sooner you get the coffee, the sooner we can get started."

In record time, he was back with three cups of coffee in the standard Styrofoam cup. "Sorry, we aren't too classy around here. No one wants to take time to wash a mug."

"Too busy catching the bad guys, eh?"

Nick changed the subject with a casual remark.

"I was hoping to see your father at the reunion, Heather. I understand he's a career Marine. I suppose with these wars the U.S. is involved in it's difficult to get away."

Heather made no immediate comment but looked into Nick's face and calmly said, "My father did attend the reunion."

Nick's brows furrowed and he stoked his chin as he recalled, "I was there for a number of hours and met everyone in the ballroom but Brock Hamilton was not among us. The MC even called out the names of all present."

Heather insisted. "My father was at the Shifting Sands Hotel. I know he sent back his RSVP because Mom was in charge of that part of it."

Seeing the doubt on Nick's face, she took a deep breath and simply continued, "My father is Coach Williams."

Nick felt as though she'd kicked him in the stomach. He stared at this woman but his mind refused to comprehend. The boys on the team had looked up to Coach Williams. Even though he wasn't that much older than the seniors he coached, he was still someone they respected. Nick's mouth tried to form words but not a sound came out. Silence chilled the air.

Finally Conner interjected. "The head coach of the Dolphin's?"

"Yes."

Nick managed to utter, "Forgive me, Heather, but every male on campus knew Lyndy was off limits. Brock idolized her and heaven help the guy who tried to separate them. Believe me I had the scars and bruises to prove it."

Heather's face softened and she asked, "May I tell you the whole story? This is what I meant this morning when we talked. I had a feeling you'd be shocked. It's a long story."

Conner pulled his chair closer. He didn't want to miss a word.

Nick gave her a nod and checked to be sure the door of his office was closed.

"We've got all day. Go ahead."

"Mom and Coach Williams had an affair. She got pregnant two months before graduation but he never knew it. She covered it up by marrying Brock right after they left school. In fact, they eloped. Broke Grandma's heart. She'd been planning her daughter's wedding from the day she was born. Big southern affair, you can imagine.

"When I arrived early, Mom told everyone I was premature but Brock wasn't fooled. He started putting two and two together and the answer was not four. He didn't want children right off. Insisted on, you know, precautions. His goal was to have a military career and get established first."

Heather paused, took a drink of coffee and continued, "When he confronted Mom, he told her there were times he'd been suspicious that something was going on between her and Coach but he was afraid of losing Mom so he dismissed it. When Mom confessed he went ballistic. Told her that my father would pay dearly for his act of indiscretion. She begged him to forgive her and for a year they put up a good front but it didn't last. He couldn't stand the sight of me - refused to support another man's child. He tried to control her every move. Sometimes it bordered on abuse. She was afraid of him. Divorce was her best option."

Conner's eyes widened and he asked, "Do you need a break?"

"It helps to talk, thank you."

Nick looked at Heather; his expression remained resolute but his emotions churned. "How do you know all this?"

"Lieutenant, a few years ago, Mom had a spiritual experience. Her whole personality changed and she confessed to me that her conscience would not bear another minute without telling me the truth. She wanted me to know who my true father was. She even wrote him and asked if he could meet us in Atlanta."

Both detectives asked simultaneously "Did he?"

Heather continued, "He came. I was twenty and skeptical. After all, most men in his situation would deny an affair with a student. Risky business, especially when it produced a daughter he knew nothing about."

Heather licked her lips and took another drink of coffee.

"Mom was a nervous wreck. The minute she saw him, the look in both of their eyes told me everything I wanted to know. Lieutenant, they loved each other. I was conceived in mutual consent. Now, don't get me wrong, I'm not advocating their behavior. It was pure sin! My mother was no saint and she admitted she used every opportunity to attract his attention.

"For the past five years I've gotten to know my father. After finding Mom again, he wanted to give me his legitimate name but mom knew if she married him, Brock would squeal to every newspaper in the county and Garrett William's career would be over. A scandalous affair between a high school coach and a senior doesn't look good on a resume, does it?

"I found an album that documented all the accolades and awards he received. From the time he first came to

Gulfview High the football team won the state championship year after year. My father became head coach within five years. College offers started rolling in but he always refused them. Now I know why."

"But who knew besides Brock and he was out of the picture?" asked Conner.

All three cups of coffee grew cold as Heather's story unfolded.

Nick held up his hand to stop her. "Do you object if we take notes? My mind's already blown away and I don't want to forget something important."

"No problem." Both men picked up their notepads and pens.

"Remember, I told you Brock swore he'd make father pay. He made good on his promise. Nothing physical. No, he took another approach. Blackmail! Plain and simple. Threatened to break the scandal wide open so not a college in the country would hire my father. Dad gave in to protect Mom. Recently, though, he told her he'd had enough and asked her if she would agree to go public if need be. She agreed. Brock knew the game was over. He's number one on my suspect list, gentlemen."

"Certainly possible," Conner concurred. "But he wasn't at the reunion."

Heather was quick to add, "He knew about it because an invitation was sent to everyone who made up the class of '86'. He may not have been at the hotel but he could've still been in town."

For a second there was silence in the room broken only by the tapping of Nick's pencil on his notepad as he gathered his thoughts. His gaze was steady; he looked into the eyes of this young woman eager to solve her mother's murder.

"Heather, I'm going to have to talk to Coach. I know this is hard to hear, but he may also be a suspect."

A gasp took her breath away and her emotions flowed like water through a broken dam. Trembling hands wiped away a stream of mascara tinted tears. Conner pulled a tissue from a box on Nick's desk and handed it to Heather.

"No way!" she finally muttered. "He could never have killed her! I know him. He was willing to give up a marriage and a career for her."

Nick continued, "Coach and I talked at the reunion. He hinted that Florida State had made him an offer. It may have been more than he could resist. With your mother gone, he could deny anything Brock might divulge. He could refuse a paternity test. I'm sorry, Heather, but I have to look at all the angles - for Lyndy's sake."

She nodded and dabbed at the sniffles. "How will I ever explain this to Grandmother? She thinks I'm Brock Hamilton's daughter. To learn that I'm an illegitimate granddaughter is the last thing she needs to know. Mom simply couldn't tell her."

"That's a call you're going to have to make," advised Conner.

Heather picked up her purse and stood. She was ready to leave. Nick's fatherly instinct made him want to reach out and give this hurting young woman a hug; but the formalities of his job required that he maintain his professional manner. "Heather, we appreciate what you've told us today. It took courage. You may have put our

investigation on a path that will help find the murderer."
He smiled. "Conner, why don't you walk Heather to her
car."

Conner jumped to his feet. "My pleasure, Boss."

Chapter Twelve

The aroma of fried chicken set his nostrils a flare the moment Nick opened the screen door. For a second, he was certain Janet must be standing over the cast iron skillet fixing his favorite meal. Instead, her apron - clad offspring gently lowered a chicken thigh into the boiling oil. The spattering grease stung her fingers but she reached for a floured breast and repeated the process. Several strands of auburn hair covered one eye but she flipped her head back in time to see her father enter the kitchen.

"Oh, hi, Dad. Didn't hear you come in."

"Well, well. And what's going on here?" Nick kissed her cheek. "Tell me I'm not imagining this. My daughter cooking! And fried chicken no less."

"Aunt Peg's idea; she told me how to do it. Not that big a deal, really."

"Secret's in the timing." commented Nick. "Cooked tender on the inside and crispy on the outside."

"Hey, sounds like you and the Colonel should have teamed up" said Penny as she poked the thigh with her long-handled fork and examined their dinner. "Hmm, still pink juices. I'm not into rare chicken."

Nick walked to the fridge, opened it and pulled out a beer. The pop of the pull tab caught Penny's attention. Her brows knit together and she asked, "Hard day? You always drink after a hard day."

Nick swallowed his first swig and answered, "Yes, it was a difficult day; I heard something I wasn't prepared to hear and it knocked me for a loop."

Curiosity replaced her concern. "Oh yeah, what was it?"

"Can't tell you; the case is still open."

"Aw, Dad, you can't just dangle bait in front of me and then yank it away." Her eyes pleaded with him. "You know I'm not going to yak it all over town."

"Ethics, sweetheart." Nick craned his neck to see the skillet. "Looks like that thigh is exactly the way your papa likes it. Missed lunch today so I'm ready even if it jumps out of the pan on its own. There is nothin' like the smell of fried chicken. Looks like you did yourself proud. Apparently, some of your mother's culinary skills did rub off on you after all."

Penny gave her father a smug grin then added, "The proof is in the taste. Grab your favorite dressing out of the fridge. I fixed a salad, too."

Half-way through the meal, their light banter turned in a different direction.

Penny put down her fork, wiped her chin with a napkin and looked at her father.

"Aunt Peg and I had a talk."

"Oh, oh, this sounds serious; especially if my big sister is involved."

"I know why Grandpa sneaks off down to the river so much."

Nick swallowed the last of his chicken and waited for Penny to continue.

"He's drinking. To try and forget. He blames himself for Uncle Ted's death doesn't he?"

" It's haunted him all these years. I've never been able to convince him it wasn't his fault."

Penny reached over and placed her hand on Nick's arm. "Gramps is not the only one I'm worried about." She stopped and let her words penetrate the silence. "I'm afraid you're going down the same path."

Taken back, Nick pulled his arm away and put up a hand to signal 'stop'. "Whoa, young lady! There's a big difference between my drinking habits and your grandfather's. An occasional beer versus a hidden stash does not indicate a problem."

"I didn't say you had a problem; but I'm concerned that it could become one. I notice that the more difficult the case, the greater the number of cans in the recycling box. I've emptied it twice this week already."

There was no point arguing with her; the evidence spoke for itself. A sheepish look preceded Nick's response, "Guilty as charged. I promise to do better. Quitting cold turkey may be more than I can handle right now, but knowing you care will make it easier."

Penny jumped from the chair and gave her father a giant bear hug.

#

Homecoming Week-end at the high school in Gulfview always lived up to everyone's expectations. Classrooms, gyms and school hallways buzzed with anticipation. Posters and banners proclaimed an anticipated win for the home team and defeat for the rivals. Football dominated everyone's minds.

The stadium grounds buzzed with practice activity; the sound of drums, cymbals and trumpets reverberated off the aluminum bleachers while band members marched in unison at one end of the field. Cheerleaders bounced, pranced and shouted as blue and gray jerseys fought team mates for control of the pigskin.

Coach Williams stood on the sidelines instructing his team on different plays that had brought triumph so many times in the past. Nick looked at this man and a dichotomy of thoughts raced around in his head. Morally, he'd crossed the line with a student, cheated on his wife and fallen for a blackmail scheme. At this moment, a team of thirty young impressionable boys respected and followed his directions to a Tee. And to top it off, his name was now high on Nick's list of murder suspects.

A whistle signaled the end of practice, and Nick walked across the field toward Williams. Although his heart was heavy, he managed to start the conversation on a light note. "Looking good, Coach. I can tell the boys want this one bad."

Both men shook hands and Coach came back with, "They're not the only ones. If we get this one tomorrow evening we'll have another shot at State."

"How many would that be for you?"

"Aw, more than I deserve, I'm sure." The modesty in his voice sounded sincere. "But you're not here to discuss games with me, are you?"

Nick looked around at the kids still milling about and lowered his voice, "Actually, I am. Can we go somewhere a little more private?"

Alarm registered on William's face and he was quick to say, "Sure, my office is right around the corner. But then you remember that, right?"

"Oh, yeah. Believe I was hauled up on the carpet a few times for messing around. Brock Hamilton and I never saw eye to eye. But then, I'm sure you remember that, right?" he said, half- joking and still trying to ease into the hard words he was about to offer.

Williams' lips pursed and a hardness in his facial expression told Nick he'd hit a nerve. "That's why I'm here, Coach. I know about Lyndy and you – including the blackmail."

"Who told you that?" he protested.

"Your daughter."

Coach dropped his head into his hands and a deep sigh followed. The next few seconds of silence seemed like an eternity but as he raised his head, the tears on his face washed away any bravado he might have shown. Nick looked into the eyes of a broken man. His voice cracked and he spoke in spurts.

"I..., I loved her, Nick." He pulled a white linen handkerchief from a back pocket, wiped his eyes and continued. "It was wrong; I'm guilty on all counts. And now she's gone." A new round of tears flowed freely; but so did words of explanation.

"I should have taken my chances and called Brock's bluff; but I desperately wanted to protect Lyndy and Heather. They meant more to me than anything a college could offer. A strange thing happened a few months ago, though."

Nick stopped writing and he asked, "What was that?"

A softness replaced the anguish on Coach's face and the tone of his voice was different. "Lyndy's personality changed. She became humbler- she no longer displayed her usual, worldly outward confidence. Instead an inner strength seemed to guide her. She told me how important truth had become to every facet of our lives and that she was ready to come clean about our past. She encouraged me to stop the blackmail; and I agreed."

Nick cleared his throat. "Coach, the detective in me has to be blunt. With Lyndy out of the picture, you can deny any accusation Brock brings against you. Even Heather's paternity. After all, they were married when she was born. And you could refuse a paternity test. So, the intimidation stops and you're free to head to Tallahassee. Until it's proven otherwise, I have to consider you a suspect."

The color drained from Coach's face; but he saw Melino's point. "All I can say is that I'm innocent. Guilty of adultery, but innocent of murder."

"Not to labor the issue, but where does your wife fit into all of this?"

"When Lyndy and I decided to come clean I confessed to Marnie. It wasn't a pretty picture; but to be honest, I think she was upset about the money more than the affair. She never was able to have children; so the fact that another woman gave me a child didn't sit well. I

96

moved into the guest room. The divorce will be final at the end of this month.

Nick frowned and said, "Been there; done that. One more thing. Where did you go when you left the reunion?"

Coach's face reddened and he hesitated before answering, "Lyndy and I agreed to meet at the dunes a couple miles down from the hotel- for old time's sake. But I never made it. A broken beer bottle a half mile from the lifeguard stand flattened my right front tire. The stupid spare was in my garage; so, I had to wait almost forty-five minutes for AAA to show up. Saturday night's must keep 'em busy. Anyway, I called Lyndy's cell; but she didn't answer."

"I'll be checking AAA's records," replied Nick. That should be easy. And we'll also be looking at cell phone records. How many times did you try to call her?"

"Several times," came the answer. "Why is that important?"

"Because," said Nick, as he stood and closed his notebook, "you still had plenty of time to walk to Lyndy's location; and if you stayed with your vehicle, as you claim, cell phone tower triangulation will confirm that you were stationary, and not taking a hike to the dunes. Sensing that Coach's story would check out, Nick stuck his notebook into the inside pocket of his jacket and rose from the chair. He extended his hand. "Hope the Dolphins do you proud, Coach. Win this one for Lyndy."

An empty, nauseous feeling settled over Williams as he watched Nick prepare to depart. Although no accusing words were spoken, Garrett saw the disappointment in his former student's eyes as details of his affair unfolded.

"None of this would have happened, Nick, if I hadn't been so weak and willing to give in to Lyndy's charms. Lyndy had this incredible power over men; but it's still my fault. I was the adult; and she was the flirtatious kid. Once she caught my eye, I entangled myself in her web; and I didn't want out. There was no comparison between her and my wife. Marnie and I married while we were still in college. Big mistake. Her feigned interest in my football career lasted maybe a year and then her ambition to become a business CEO took us in different directions. I wanted a divorce but she begged me to stay. Claimed it would hurt her career by making her look unstable. The truth is, we were living separate lives from day one, and didn't even know it."

The longer Coach dwelled on the interview, the further he sank into depression. *Now I'm shadowed by the suspicion of murder.* He couldn't deny that with Lyndy gone, it opened up the possibility of a career in the college leagues. But at his age, he needed to take action; because those opportunities would dry up quickly. One thing he knew for sure. For the time being, Nick Melino had him in his sights.

Chapter Thirteen

The last rays of a setting sun ushered in evening shadows as Nick drove into his garage. A squeaking door hinge reminded him he needed to buy another can of WD 40 to put a stop to that irritating noise. As he stepped across the threshold Penny called out, "Where have you been? I was starving so I guess you're eating alone tonight. Aunt Peggy sent down a pot roast and I couldn't wait a minute longer. It's divine."

"Sounds like I might be lucky if there's any left." Nick brushed his lips against the top of her head.

"So what held you up tonight, Dad?"

"Just left the court house. Been there most of the day. That robbery at the Bait and Tackle finally got on the docket. Justice prevailed; the guy's going to prison, but I had to testify. And those defense lawyers like to put on their dog and pony show. So I couldn't leave."

"I feel as though I've been cemented to this chair, too," Penny offered. "Big paper due tomorrow. I have to read this 1700 century play called "The Mourning Bride" then compare the heroine to a modern day woman.

"Sounds uplifting," mocked Nick.

"This old English is killing me. Listen to this."

Before Penny could take another breath, Nick interrupted, " Sweetheart, I will understand these old masters much better on a full stomach. Let me stuff myself with roast beef and then, I'm all ears."

Forty-five minutes later Penny looked up from her literature book to see a relaxed transformed father coming down the stairs. No longer in a suit and tie, he looked comfortable in jeans and a sweat shirt.

"Settle in, Dad; it's like a new language." Penny commenced to reading aloud,

"Heaven has no rage, like love to hatred turned,
Nor hell a fury like a woman scorned."

Nick raised his eyebrows and commented, "H-e-a-v-y. Glad it's you interpreting the meaning, Honey. I've been listening to too much rhetoric from the lawyers and witnesses for one day. Has my brain fogged."

"Actually, Dad, modern scholars have changed the original last line to say —"Hell hath no fury like a woman scorned." Sounds better to me."

"Penny," Nick said as his interest peeked, "Read that last line again, please."

"Hell hath no fury like a woman scorned."

A smile lit up Nick's face. "You just might have put me on the trail of another suspect in the McNeil case."

"Who?" questioned Penny, wide-eyed and curious. One look at her father's expression; and she knew the answer. "Okay, okay. Confidential information. I get it!"

#

The line of customers at the Southern Community Credit Union wound around the stiles like a proverbial snake. Nick scanned the waiting crowd and decided that the three tellers had their hands full enough without his intrusion. *Must be the end of the month- pay day.* For a second, panic tightened the muscles in his stomach. *Did I remember to make the mortgage payment this month? Automatic withdrawal, Nick. When are you going to join the twenty-first century? How many times had he heard that line from Janet? She's right; gotta get it set up. Too many things on my mind these days.*

Besides, since his police business was not with the tellers, Nick found the information desk and asked, "May I see Mrs. Williams, please? She's expecting me."

After a moment's pause, the receptionist scanned her appointment book, smiled and instructed, "Third door on your right."

"Thank you."

The nameplate attached to the glass panel read, Marnie Williams, Assistant Manager. Before Nick curled his fingers to knock, a woman in her early forties, dressed in a business suit ushered him into her office. She removed the stylish glasses that sat half-way down her nose. Fine lines emphasized sober thin lips that refused to smile.

With a wave of her hand, she motioned for Nick to sit down. He suddenly felt like a school boy who'd been sent to see the principal.

"Well, Lieutenant, since we've not had a robbery at this branch this morning, I assume you have something else you'd like to discuss."

"I do, Ma'am. Did your husband tell you that he and I talked about Lyndy McNeil's death yesterday?"

The muscles in her cheeks grew taut and her body stiffened.

"We converse very little these days. I heard all I needed to a few weeks ago. I'm sure he told you the whole sordid story. The day I sign the final divorce papers will be the happiest day of my life. Good thing for her I didn't go to the reunion, I would have clawed her eyes out!"

Nick struggled to keep a straight face. *Not a doubt in my mind, lady.*

"There was always a third person in our marriage, Lieutenant - an invisible one. A woman can sense these things. Never could prove it, though. Garrett covered his tracks well." Marnie maintained her offensive posture. "Told me those trips to Atlanta were conferences - football, coaching, school related. I bought into it. They say the wife is always the last to know."

Marnie pushed back strands of highlighted hair that fell against eyes that betrayed her feelings of defeat and anger. In a voice that sounded disconnected and almost lifeless she asked, "So what does her death have to do with me?"

Nick held nothing back. "You had motive to kill her." He waited for the words to register and then proceeded with his questioning. "Where were you the night Lyndy McNeil was murdered?"

"Sitting on my pool deck. Sleep hasn't come easily for me since my marriage fell apart. And at my age starting over isn't easy. So many decisions to make. Too much on my mind. Nothing could have made me sleep then. I remember it was a moonlit night; and even though I didn't really care, something inside of me compelled me to keep waiting for the sound of Garrett's car in the driveway. Habit, I guess. Anyway, I did eventually go back to bed – not sure when. The next morning he told me he had a flat. But to make a long story short, Lieutenant, I didn't kill her. Marnie's lips curled into a sneer. "I guess someone else hated her as much as I did."

Hell hath no fury like a woman scorned continued to echo in the back of Nick's mind as he extended his hand, "Thank you for your time, Mrs. Williams."

Marnie Williams sat trance-like for several minutes as the words of Lieutenant Melino registered in her tired brain. She never thought of herself as a suspect in Lyndy's murder but she could see why the investigators would point a finger at her. If the truth be known, she probably did kill the woman in her sub conscience - more than once. Every time she imagined Garrett cheating on her and letting that conniving Brock Hamilton take away money that belonged to them bitterness welled up inside of her. Make no mistake, she'd get the money back. Her divorce lawyer was the best in the business. Garrett would pay for his indiscretions and there would be nothing left to share with Lyndy – not that that mattered anymore.

Chapter Fourteen

The first week in November came in with a last blast of election rhetoric and campaign slurs from every direction one looked. The TV at the Sandspur Bar and Grill, usually tuned to the sports channel, showed nothing but one political ad after another. Martin McNeil's face dominated the airways.

Andrews took a long drink from a Miller bottle and looked at Meyers and Melino before asking, "So is our local yokel going to claim the Senate seat, guys?"

Meyers was quick to respond. "Not with my vote. I like what I've heard from that woman from Crestview."

Nick jiggled the ice in his glass of soda. "The newspaper article on McNeil's gambling was his death sentence. This county's too conservative to tolerate that kind of behavior from a Senator."

Both partners nodded their heads in agreement as Nick continued, "I'll know by morning if the party's over for him and I plan to pay him another visit. So far, he's put me off every time I come near. Either of you free to tag along? He's had all these months to polish his spin; so, I could use an extra pair of eyes and ears."

Andrews volunteered, "Count me in. I know how slick he can be."

#

One look at McNeil's headquarters told the story. The somber look on the young workers' faces as they ripped banners, posters, and sagging, popped balloons from windows and walls was enough to announce their candidate's utter defeat.

This time, two detectives waited for Martin's arrival, feeling comfortable in the knowledge that his political days were probably over.

"Let's get this over with, Melino. As you can see this is not the best day of my life," Marin growled, as he stormed into the room.

"I understand, Sir. A politician's life rests in the vote of the people, doesn't it? You take a chance that the odds will be in your favor, right?"

Martin's face tensed. "Is this your subtle way of asking about my alleged gambling debts? Ever since that newspaper article you've dogged me like a shadow."

Andrews pulled out his notepad, poised and ready to write.

"I'm more concerned about who killed your sister than I am with your debts and poor investment choices," Nick returned. "Your gambling buddies play rough; and Lyndy inherited a fortune. With her gone, in time, you'd stand to gain the whole estate. Or, perhaps her murder could be used to communicate a serious threat to you.

Wouldn't you agree, Sir?" Nick looked for any change in Martin's demeanor, but he was stone faced. "My guess is that your mother will take a kinder attitude toward your foibles than your father did. A mother's heart tends to keep forgiving, you know."

"We all have our vices, Lieutenant. Murder is not one of mine." Martin's voice grew cold. " Even my ole man was not the saint folks painted him to be."

Nick's raised eyebrows coaxed more from Martin. "Women were his weakness. Mom knew; but southern ladies are expert at turning the other cheek when it comes to their husbands' indiscretions."

Andrew's pen never left the paper as he asked, "You have proof of that; and what's the connection to your sister's death?"

"Yes, I've got proof alright. And I'll leave it to you to make the connection."

"What kind?"

"DNA." Martin sat back in his chair. A smug grin on his face challenged Nick.

"DNA? Whose? And why are you telling us this?"

"Revenge, I suppose. Dad ruined me. My reputation's been smeared; and I put my last dime into a losing political battle. And, now, you suspect I killed my sister."

"Okay, let's get back on track with the DNA," suggested Andrews.

"I've been suspicious for years that I have a half-sister. Dad's personal secretary was a little too personal in my opinion. I may have been young when I came into the company but I wasn't blind and stupid. She told everyone her husband was shipped to Vietnam, and that a couple months before she gave birth to a girl, he had stepped on a mine and died. Last year, I did a little detective work on my own. Even made a trip to the Wall, you know, the Vietnam Memorial in Washington. Not a trace of a Gary Bradford anywhere on that slab of granite. I'm convinced it was a lie; a cover-up for dear ole Dad's misbehavior. He was so good with double standards!"

Martin stopped and took a drink from a bottle of water.

"Why don't you ask her? Your father's gone now," suggested Andrews.

"Can't. Cancer got to her five years ago. So, a few months ago I told her daughter about my suspicion and asked if she'd consent to have our hair follicles tested for DNA. I have a friend at a private lab and the results would have been our little secret." Martin paused while both detectives leaned forward to hear the result.

"Alana, now Perkins, the secretary's daughter is my half-sister!"

Nick dropped his pen and his gasp broke the silence.

"Thought you'd be surprised, Lieutenant." Martin gave a mocking laugh. "Amazing what goes on behind closed doors isn't it?

As Nick regained his composure, he looked at Martin and said, "This is all very interesting, but, as far as Lyndy's case is concerned, you're still a suspect.

"And the burden of proof is on you, Melino." Martin's lips curled into an all-to- familiar sneer. "Now, if you'll excuse me, gentlemen, I have more important work to do."

108

Chapter Fifteen

The change of seasons from summer to fall chased the humidity out of the stifling air and clear skies reigned in North West Florida. A morning chill greeted early risers and energized folks eager to complete tasks put aside because of summer heat.

Nick never had the luxury of postponing chores, and he worked long hours trying to reduce the number of cases still pending. He'd lost track of the number of times he'd read Lyndy's file. Did he miss something? Yes, he had suspects, but so far no hard evidence that any of them might be guilty of foul play. Frustration met him at every corner. To top it off, the owner of the convenience store turned out to be an illegal who fled the country and took the key to the safety deposit box with him.

Sure would like to get my hands on that surveillance tape. It's a long-shot but one never knows when little things can lead to something important. Looks like a court order's needed this time.

Nick's eyes scrutinized the list of classmates who'd responded to the reunion RSVP. Brock Hamilton's name was checked off but he had not shown up at the hotel. Why did he renege?

Nick reached for the city phone book and looked under listings for 'Hamilton'. 'Hamilton' surnames took up a quarter of the page but Nick's finger went down the list until he found Howard, Brock's father.

The ole fella's still alive - saw him at the gas station last week.

The voice that answered Nick's call was weak but audible. "Hello."

"Mr. Hamilton, this is Nick Melino, I ran into you at the filling station the other day."

"I remember; you're the detective. You played football with my son."

"Yes, sir. Speaking of Brock, do you recall if he was home the end of the first week of September?"

"I sure do. It was his last R& R before he shipped out for Afghanistan. His voice grew stronger with excitement. "Took me fishing out in the Gulf. Caught the biggest Grouper I ever hauled in. Was right tasty, too."

"They don't get any better, I agree." Nick continued to dig. "Did he happen to mention his high school reunion? It was held at the Shifting Sands Hotel on the beach."

Nick waited while the elder man paused and thought about the question. Finally, he said, "I believe he did mention it; in fact he dressed in his uniform. He's proud to be a Marine - always been a tough guy."

"Mr. Hamilton, I was at the reunion and your son was not there."

"Hmm," a moment of silence followed. "that's where he was headed when he left me. Another pause. "No, I'm wrong. First he went to Biloxi. Said he had some business with some guy in his outfit. You never know with Brock what he's up too. Told me not to wait up. Figured it'd be a late night seein' his old football buddies and all."

Nick started to thank him for his time when Howard's tone changed. "Hey, Detective, why are you asking me all these questions? You think he had somethin' to do with that McNeil woman's murder? They ain't had nothin' to do with each other in over twenty years."

And for Brock's sake, thought Nick, *you better hope it stayed that way.* "Just checkin', Sir. Take care. Appreciate talking to you."

Nick hung up the phone and mentally added another unanswered question to his list. *Where were you the night of September seventh, Brock Hamilton? And what were you doing? You certainly wouldn't be inconspicuous in your uniform! Someone had to see you; and I'll find out who did!*

September 7, 2011

Brock Hamilton was on his third tour of duty fighting a war in a country he couldn't have named twenty years ago. He lived and breathed the military. The slogan, 'A Few Good Men' caught his attention in high school and he knew exactly where his future lay. His tough demeanor on the football field aided by an egotistic attitude gave him an edge the Marines were happy to recruit. It didn't hurt that he claimed the "Star-Quarter-back" title and held it until graduation. Marrying Lyndy McNeil wasn't in his game plan; at least not so soon; but, her powers of persuasion could wilt any man's defenses. Little did he know that the marriage would turn out to be a sham, a cover-up for a kid that wasn't his. He'd tried to put the truth behind him; but every time he looked at that baby, all he saw was Coach messin' with his Lyndy. She belonged to him - not anyone else!

The invitation to attend the class of '86' reunion couldn't have come at a better time. Although they hadn't spoken for years, Brock welcomed the opportunity to see his ex-wife again. This sudden decision by Garrett to stop sending monthly checks put a crimp in his lifestyle. He needed the money to supplement his 'business' income. Opium plants in Afghanistan produced the product he needed to supply the habits of men who came home from a war wasted and addicted. But he needed more income than his business provided. Perhaps his new customer would improve his bottom line. A quick trip to the Biloxi airport to deliver the goods to his man and he'd be back by the time the reunion party was in full swing.

A devious smirk creased the edges of Brock's lips as he drove along Interstate 10 thinking of Lyndy. *She can change the spots on a leopard! Coach is putty in her hands. All it'll take is a little reminder of her past behavior and how small town tongues like to spread gossip. She wouldn't want to embarrass the family, especially now that her brother's running for Senator. By the time I'm finished with her, she'll be begging Williams to get back in line. Oh, yes, I'll be having a little persuasive chat with Lyndy.*

Chapter Sixteen

Anytime the Seminoles and the Gators met on the football field the atmosphere became electric. Days before the actual competition, sparks of fan loyalty ignited one conversation after another. And staffers at the Sheriff's Office were not immune to all of the boasting and banter.

"Hey, Melino," Andrews bellowed down the hallway, "Wait up. Got any plans for Saturday evening?"

Nick thought for a moment, and then shrugged his shoulders. "Not really; Penny's driving over to Jacksonville to see her mom. Course, the big games on; so, I don't want to miss seeing the Gators whip Florida State." He gave Conner a slap on the back.

"In your dreams, pal. Not with the defense we've got this year."

"Sure! So what's your impending humiliation got to do with my future plans?"

"Gonna have a tail-gate barbeque at my place and then watch the game on that new flat screen I bought last week. A few of the guys are coming over. If you're interested bring whatever you want to throw on the grill. I'll handle the rest. You're a Budweiser man, right?"

"None other. Sounds good to me; and I need a break. This McNeil case has had me running around in circles. Been rackin' my brain night and day. I sure wanted to have it wrapped up before the New Year."

"It'll happen when we least expect it. We're missing that one piece of the puzzle but sooner or later someone's gonna slip up. They always do. I'm still watching Martin's every move."

"Admire your optimism, Partner. Keep it up. Say, how 'bout I bring a couple pounds of the Gulf's finest jumbo shrimp. My secret spices will knock your socks off! Believe it or not," Nick chuckled, "it was the one thing I did that suited Janet."

"My mouth's watering already," said Andrews. "Don't forget now - tomorrow around five."

#

With the week-end starting, Nick knew there'd be a run on seafood. *Better drive over to Alana's shop before they're all sold out. Been meaning to drop in on her to see how she's doing. I understand how it hurts to lose your best friend.*

Nick hadn't seen Alana since Lyndy's funeral. He didn't think much of it at the time; but now, he recalled how she entwined herself around the family during this ordeal. Before Heather arrived, it was Alana who spent time with Katherine at the McNeil home and Nick saw her sit with them during the service. Maybe Martin's story was true? Did Lyndy know she had a half sister? How would that little secret affect their relationship? All of these questions ran through Nick's mind as he pulled up in front of a neon sign advertising Southern Shores Seafood.

The tinkle of a small bell above the door announced his arrival and the sweet smell of fresh seafood set his stomach rumbling. No fishy odor here. It was these quality goods that kept bringing him back.

A knee-length apron covered Alana's slim body; and her dark hair, pulled back in a French twist was secured with a tortoise shell barrette. Now Nick saw her through new eyes. Yes, there was a resemblance -- not to Lyndy, but to Martin.

At first, she didn't notice Nick's presence while she waited on a customer, but as she closed the cash register she called out. "Hey, Nick. Good to see you. I've tried to call your office to see if there's been any progress on Lyndy's murder but..." she caught her breath and lowered her eyes, "you know, I find it hard to even think about it."

"I know how you feel but I have to think about it all the time. It's my job. In fact it consumes me. Off the record," Nick hushed his tone, "it's a tough one. Little progress."

"Does this mean it's going to end up in the cold case file?"

"Not if I can help it."

"Well," Alana changed the subject, "what can I get for you today? Mike brought in a fresh load of shrimp not two hours ago."

"Jumbos?"

"Your favorite."

"Two pounds. Football party tomorrow evening and I intend to provide the best part of the meal!"

"Sounds like a blast. Love these pigskin parties; great for business." Alana smiled as she packaged Nick's purchase. "Here," she said, picking up a glass stein, proudly pointing to the Southern Shores logo and placing it in a separate bag. "For our special customers. Never hurts to advertise."

"Hey, thanks. Something tells me it'll be put to good use. Take care, friend, and keep your ear to the ground for me, ya hear?"

Alana nodded and gave him a thumbs up as he closed the shop's door.

Since Penny left Friday afternoon to travel to Jacksonville, the Saturday chores fell on Nick's shoulders. Gone were the days when he puttered around his garage, picked up his clubs and headed for the golf course or called his dad to go fishing. Instead, even with his daughter's help, laundry, vacuuming, and grocery shopping demanded top priority. The more he took on the role of 'Mr. Mom', the more he appreciated the challenges facing a working mother. *I probably didn't give Janet enough credit. Too self-absorbed in my own career. Hindsight! Down right depressing!"* Nick looked at his watch as he pulled the last of the bed sheets from the dryer. Conner expected him in another hour. *"Oh, well, nothin' like a football game, good food and his favorite suds to bring a man out of the doldrums. Andrews, you saved the day."*

Dressed in jeans, a shirt sporting the Gator's insignia and a blue and orange cap, there was no mistaking his allegiance. His team may not win the game but at least he'd have done his part.

The sound of a yapping Jack Russell dog running in circles around his neighbor caught Nick's attention the minute he opened his front door. At the first sight of Nick, Tinkerbell bolted away from Les, ran through the spray from the sprinkler system and proceeded to jump at the bowl of shrimp Nick held in his hand.

A gruff command boomed through the air. "Tinkerbell, get over here!"

Accustomed to his master's voice, the dog turned in midair and dashed across the property line trampling a bed of petunias.

"Dad blasted dog!" shouted Les giving her a swat on her hind end before looking at Nick. "If Lucy didn't love that animal more' an me I'd have it down to the pound before you could wink an eye. Hyper-active doesn't even come close to describing that canine."

"No harm done; the shrimp are still intact."

"Ahh, let me guess." Les gave Nick the once over. " Gator colors, man food -- must be a game gatherin' tonight."

"Right on, pal. My partner's having a few guys over. Gonna kick back a little. Been a busy week."

Les slapped Nick on the back as he lowered his voice, "Have one for me; Lucy never did take to me drinkin' beer. Women! Born to spoil a man's fun, I reckon."

"Hey, she's just keeping you in line, friend. After forty years, it's worked hasn't it?"

Les laughed as he grabbed Tinkerbell and hoisted her up in his arms. "Let me hang onto this un' while you back out. Next thing she'll be racin' after you down the street."

Nick slid behind the wheel, waved good-by and drove into the setting sun.

The smell of hamburgers and chicken grilling on the barbeque set hunger pangs gnawing in Nick's empty stomach the second he emerged from his car. Meyers spotted him and signaled for Nick to come around the side of the house to the back patio.

"Got any room left on that thing for the Gulf's finest shrimp?" Nick asked.

Conner flipped another burger into a warming tray and pushed aside a chicken thigh. "Always, Boss. Been waiting all day to sink my teeth into those jumbos. Grab a Bud on your way past the cooler, too."

"Say, where'd you get shrimp that size?" asked Tony, another member of the detective team.

"Southern Shores Seafood. Mike and Alana Perkins own it."

"Isn't she the gal who was friends with Lyndy McNeil? How's she handling it?"

"I get the impression she's still pretty upset. We talked some when I was in the shop on Friday. I had no idea they could get shrimp that size."

Conner gave everyone the time-out sign and said, "Fellas, no! no! no! Tonight we leave our work at the Office. No one is on duty here; so turn off your cell phones." A smug grin inched across his lips as he continued, "The only thing on our minds tonight is the fact that the Gators are going to take a beating."

With that remark, three of the eight men gave Andrews a good-natured 'Swamp' chomp and a round of laughter and applause followed.

By six o'clock, with plates heaped with potato salad, baked beans, shrimp, chicken, hamburger and a can of brew, each man settled in front of the flat screen TV to satisfy not only his hunger but his longing to see his team win. Each time either side made a touchdown, it was celebration rounds for everyone. By the third quarter, the Gators had six touchdowns to their credit and Nick was beginning to feel light headed. His eyes strained to focus on the moving figures on the screen and every now and then he felt a pulsating sensation behind his right temple. Finally, a deafening roar went up from not only the stadium but in Conner's living room as the last seconds of the game proved the Gators triumphant.

Confident he could drive the ten minute route to his home, Nick bade his peers goodnight and drove within the speed limit to Willow Lane. He was a few hundred feet from his driveway when a streak of white dashed out from the curb in front of him and disappeared. *What was that? Cat? Dog? Skunk?* A sudden bump accompanied by a whelping sound sent his foot to the brake. His tires screeched on the pavement as the Camaro came to an abrupt stop. A chilling vision caused his hands to momentarily freeze on the steering wheel. *No, not Tinkerbell!*

Nick grabbed a flashlight from the consul, swung the door open and with unsteady steps walked to the front of the car. As he got down on his knees to look, he recognized the whimpering of Les's dog. Fearful eyes stared back at him as a beam of light confirmed the dog's identity. Within an instant, a wave of nausea swept through Nick's body. Tinkerbell lay on her side licking a bloody misshapen left leg and paw.

"What have I done?" he muttered to himself. Shaken, Nick headed toward his neighbor's home to inform Les he'd run over his wife's favorite pet.

"Can't tell you how sorry I am. All I saw was a flash of white and then there was a thud under the car."

Les gave Nick a reassuring pat on the shoulder. "Don't blame yourself. I let her out to do her business just as you came down the street. Should've been watching her. Lucy usually takes her for a walk before bed but she's visitin' her sister in Mobile. Better go check out the damage."

While Les directed, Nick managed to maneuver his car around Tinkerbell without injuring her further but there was no doubt she needed to see a vet.

Feeling guilty, Nick offered to drive to the animal clinic but Les was quick to respond. "No offense, friend, but you don't need to be on the road tonight. Wouldn't look too good if one of our best detectives was given a DUI Take my advice; and hit the sack."

Nick's sheepish look gave way to a confession. "You've got a point. Looks like I fell off the wagon tonight." One hand reached over and stroked the back of Tinkerbell's head as she lay cradled in Les's arms. "Wish you knew, girl, how badly I feel 'bout this. Send the vet bill to me, Les. I mean it."

The blinking red light on the answering machine sent a chill through Nick as he stepped into the foyer. He dreaded late night calls. Throughout his career, he'd answered his share and they never brought good news. The throbbing in his temple intensified as he pushed the playback button and heard a stranger's voice.

"Mr. Melino, this is Tallahassee General Hospital. Your daughter, Penny Melino was brought into the emergency room at eight-thirty p.m. with a broken arm and minor lacerations. According to the police she was hit by a drunk driver. Please contact us at 805-1672."

Nick stared at the machine, his knees grew weak and his body started to tremble. *No, not my baby. She needs me. Got to get over there. But how? Les is right; I can't drive.* Fear gripped Nick as he cursed his negligent behavior. *Peggy. Peggy can drive.* He closed his eyes and willed his sister's number into his numbed brain.

She answered on the third ring. "Hello."

"Sis, I need your help." Even years of hardened experience could not dispel the emotion in his plea. "Penny's been hurt. She's in the hospital in Tallahassee." A gasp from Peggy echoed through the phone lines. "I've been out with the boys tonight and I'm in no condition to drive."

"Figures," she scolded. "I'll be right over." There were no good-byes.

Another call to the hospital put Nick in touch with the doctor on call. His assurance that Penny was in no danger calmed his jangled nerves and he walked into his bathroom, brushed his teeth and swished some mouth wash around in an attempt to mask any beer breath.

A beep of a horn announced Peggy's arrival. Nick checked his back pocket for his billfold, grabbed his house key off the counter and slammed the door on his way out.

Before he had time to close the car door, Peggy began questioning. "What happened? Is she hurt bad? I thought she went to Jacksonville."

"There was a message on the machine from the hospital. I just got off the phone with the ER doctor. Broken arm, some cuts and bruises. Shaken up, of course.

Got side-swiped by a drunk driver. Thinks it was some college dude coming back from the game."

Peggy gave her brother a side-ways glance. "Somebody else doing a little too much celebrating, eh? Here." She handed him a thermos of coffee. "It's not fresh. Left over from dinner but you need to sober up and clear that head of yours. I swear, between you and Dad you'll have me in an early grave worrying about the two of you. I had high hopes, Brother, that Dad's weakness would have helped chart a different course for you."

Nick swallowed a mouthful of coffee before responding. "It sneaks up on a person, Sis. No one wants to admit they have a problem with alcohol. Not until it hits home. I think it has tonight. I have another confession."

"Good heavens, how much can I take in one night? What is it?"

Nick hesitated a moment as though the words refused to leave his lips. "I…I almost killed Les's dog."

"Tinkerbell!" You ran over Tinkerbell?"

"I didn't see her. A flash of white disappeared under my car and then an awful thud. Les took her to the animal clinic. I'm sure her leg's broken." Beads of sweat pooled on Nick's brow and he wiped his hand across his forehead. "Jeez, Peg, what if it had been a kid? And my own daughter - booze could have killed her! I know the stats; I work with them." Nick's shoulders drooped and resignation humbled his speech. "I got my wake-up call. I promise you, it won't be easy but it's time I got a grip."

Peggy reached over and squeezed his arm. "That's my hard-nosed brother. Now, recline that seat and get some sleep. It's three and a half hours before we get to

Tallahassee, and something tells me it's going to be a long night."

Chapter Seventeen

As the lights of Tallahassee woke Nick from an uneasy sleep, he shook the grogginess from his head and looked around. Peggy smiled, "Feelin' better? We made good time; not much traffic this time of night. The GPS helped too. One more left turn and we should be at the hospital. Sure beats trying to read a folded map. Wouldn't take much to get turned in the wrong direction in this place! Maybe that's part of what's wrong with our politicians over here – too many wrong-way streets. Most of them don't have a clue what they're doing or where they're going. Thank the good God above that Martin McNeil isn't our senator. I do not trust that man!"

Nick let his opinionated sister's remark go unchallenged. He knew better than to get her started on politics. Although he privately conceded he agreed with her about McNeil.

The emergency room in this hospital resembled the ones that Nick had many occasions to visit from the time he joined the Sheriff's team up to the present. Anxious, hurting and scared men, women and children sat waiting their turn for medical attention. Ambulance sirens, ringing phones, PA announcements, and overlapping chatter all added to the uneasy commotion.

Nick and Peggy were ushered into an observation area where they found Penny medicated and sleeping. A short wait later, a doctor entered the room, fatigue written all over his forty-plus face. A quick look at his nametag and Nick extended his hand to greet him. "Dr. Murphy, I'm Nick Melino and this is my sister, Peggy. Rough night, huh?"

"Always is on game night. Crowds get carried away -- drink too much. Think they're invincible. They end up here. Unfortunately, your daughter caught the brunt of a young man's misbehavior. She's a lucky lady; it could have been a lot worse." Chills accompanied by guilt ran through Nick's body like an electric shock.

"I'm keeping her here 'til morning. If no complications arise, you can take her home."

"Doctor, I'd like to talk to the officers who were at the scene. I assume they left a name and number."

"Check at the front desk."

Before he could continue, the PA system interrupted with, "Dr. Murphy, room four."

Again, Nick offered his hand in appreciation and watched as the doctor scurried away, his white coat flapping around him.

While Penny waited to be released, Nick drove to the police station and picked up a copy of the accident report along with the name of the garage where her car had been towed. According to the officer at the scene, the SUV went through a red light and broadsided her Saturn. As is often the case, the driver, inebriated, suffered nothing but a DUI, some temporary embarrassment, and escalating insurance premiums. The sight of the mangled front end and caved in left side chilled Nick to the bone. Lucky? It was more like a miracle that she walked away with minor injuries. *That's one tough car, and that's one tough girl!* A call to the insurance company confirmed that an adjuster would get back with him.

With his faculties back to normal, Nick's second nature kicked in and questions raced through his mind begging for answers. *Why was Penny on the Interstate at nine o'clock at night? Had she called her mother; and if so, where was she? And why hadn't Penny contacted him?*

The whole story unfolded on their return trip to Gulfview. While Penny settled in the back seat, Nick got behind the wheel and listened to his daughter's explanation.

"Dad, I know I told you I was spending the week-end with mom but I have a biology exam on Monday and the more I thought about it, the more I realized I hadn't studied enough. So, I needed to get home. My plan was to spend all day today memorizing the molecular structure of a frog or whatever."

"You're too vulnerable to be traveling alone at night on the Interstate." Fatherly concern was tinged with disgust. "And, I can't believe your mother let you go."

"She tried to reason with me but you know everyone says I'm my father's daughter. Stubborn." A twinkle in Penny's eye turned into a smile that always melted Nick's heart.

"Did the hospital contact her?" asked Peggy adjusting her seatbelt.

"They did. But she's on crutches herself. Twisted her ankle playing tennis; so she couldn't drive over. Dad, I called you on your cell, but got no response. That's not like you to turn it off. What's up?"

"Conner had a game gathering and insisted we leave business at the door. That included no cell calls; especially during the game." Nick gave Penny a look of reassurance. "I promise. That's the last time I'll listen to him!"

"So who won?"

Peggy reached toward the radio and turned up the volume. "Hear it for yourself; sounds like the Seminoles are already whining." The usual banter between commentators didn't interest Nick until a familiar name gave him reason to perk up and listen.

"After last night's defeat," the announcer explained, "Florida State announced today that Coach Garrett Williams from Gulfview has accepted an offer to join the Seminoles. I understand they've been after this guy for a long time. He has an outstanding record of winning State championships for Gulfview High. Welcome aboard Coach Williams."

Everyone in the car was stunned. Nick's reaction was, "Well, I'll be …. Privately the detective in him was thinking, *just like I told him in his office, with Lyndy gone, he's free to dispute any accusation about an affair.*

Chapter Eighteen

The Sheriff's Office was all abuzz as Coach Williams reported eminent departure from Gulfview drew all sorts of opinions. Some felt he owed allegiance to the high school while others were eager to see his talents used on a larger scale at the college level. Nick offered no comment but his suspicions lingered in the background.

Meyers caught up with Nick as he left the lounge with his third coffee of the morning. Their week-end fiasco still left remnants of an unrelenting headache.

"Nick, I convinced Judge Morris to give us a court order to get hold of the surveillance tape from the In and Out store on the beach."

"Good work." A smile was followed by a triumphant thumbs up sign. "The last they told us was that no one had a key to the safe so take a locksmith with you. I want our team watching this tape together. We can't let anything slip by. It wouldn't be the first time a video camera held the secret we're looking for."

"It should be in your office by this afternoon," replied Meyers. " I'll spread the word."

Later, six men sat around a table, their eyes fixed on the TV screen.

"Any trouble getting the tape?" asked Andrews.

" No problem. They're most obliging; or more like scared to death we're going to start checking for legal alien cards since the owner high-tailed it over the border. Actually they gave me two tapes, one for outside and the other for the inside."

Meyers pressed the remote and the exterior of the convenience store popped into view, with superimposed text indicating time and date. Nick shuffled through the file marked McNeil and pulled out a sheet of paper titled tire prints.

"Okay, fellas, you're looking for a Dodge Ram, Ford mini van, a Galant and a Chevy Malibu or anything else suspicious.

Watching a surveillance tape required a keen eye and much patience. Since the time span covered six a.m. September 6 to two a.m. September 7, Nick made a suggestion.

"Meyers, fast forward to midnight. I believe that's the time period we're most interested in."

"Thanks, Boss," moaned one of the younger members of the team. "Pretty boring stuff. Not like we're watching Die Hard."

"Get used to it, Collins! This technology is a God-send. There's no disputing what the camera sees."

The minutes ticked by on the screen and when twelve-twenty a.m. came up Andrews yelled, "Pause the tape. Dodge Ram just pulled up on the right."

All eyes focused on the vehicles as each man searched for a clue that could help solve the case.

"Continue," ordered Nick.

The driver's door opened and in clear view a magnetic sign read "Southern Shores Seafood." *Who was behind the wheel? Mike or Alana?* Blood rushed to Nick's temple and his heartbeat quickened.

There was no missing the class reunion theme of Alana's tee-shirt as she hopped out of the truck and rushed into the store.

"Hey, Nick, Southern Shores Seafood. Isn't that the place your friend owns? Where you bought those super shrimp for the barbeque?" asked another detective.

"Right. Let's not jump to conclusions here. We'll be checking out her tire prints against the ones we have from the parking area. Meyers, change tapes. I want to see why she's in there."

The camera scanned up one aisle and down another as though spying on each customer. Finally, Alana grabbed a package of batteries and stood in line at the checkout counter. One foot tapped impatiently and the intense look on her face puzzled Nick. A few hours earlier, her body language had spoken of laughter and good times. She fumbled in her purse for a wallet, gave the clerk a bill and stuffed the change in her pocket of her Capri's. In seconds she ran out the door, jumped into her truck and backed into the darkness. The tape did not reveal whether she turned left or right.

Nick looked at his team. Did any of them see something he might have missed?

"Let's look at what we know," he said. "A Dodge Ram was at the beach parking lot. Alana Perkins drives a Dodge Ram. Is it the same one? Andrews get right on that and take that fellow from the tire shop with you. He seems to know what he's doing."

"I'm out of here." Andrews pushed back his chair and slipped on his jacket.

Nick crossed his arms and bit at his lower lip while he pondered for the next few seconds. "Meyers play back the part where she appeared to pick up a pack of batteries. When you get to it pause; I want to identify the size."

Images flashed backwards on the screen until someone called. "Stop. It's right here."

Once again, Nick scrutinized the familiar face and saw a look that was totally foreign to the Alana he knew. Why was she buying batteries at a convenience store?

"Looks like size D to me," piped up one detective. "Can't make out the printing but the carton looks as though it holds four D's."

"I agree," another detective responded.

"Collins, go back to the In and Out and check on that display. Remember she removed the batteries from the third row. Call me to confirm if we're right."

"Looks like I'm off to the beach, gentlemen." A teasing smile revealed a dimple on his left cheek. " You gotta love this job." He slapped his buddy on the back as he headed for the door.

#

Tom, the owner of the tire shop, agreed to accompany Andrews to Southern Shores Seafood to take a look at the Ram's tires.

"I'm going to have to get a court order to make a cast but unless I can prove sufficient cause, the judge may turn me down," Andrews said to Tom. " But, with the video and your expert opinion I believe she'll give us the go-ahead."

"Always some kind of red tape, eh? No wonder it takes so long to see justice done in this country."

Fifteen minutes later, Andrews pulled into the shop's small parking area. Not a vehicle was in sight. A large sign in the window read 'closed'.

"Just my luck," he sighed. "More wasted time. Sorry about that, Tom."

"Hey, the guy's a shrimper, right?"

Andrews nodded.

"What are the chances he's out on his boat. Let's check the marina. A lot of those guys have their own parking spots."

"What have we got to lose?" Andrews shifted gears and took off toward the gulf.

The emerald green water sparkled under a clear November sky; and as they approached the marina, sea gulls squawked and tussled over any fish remains left by the charter boats.

"Can't blame a guy for closing shop and spending his time out there." Tom motioned toward the water. "Sure is a pretty sight. I never get tired of it. Changes every day."

"No argument from this southern boy. Say, think I'll talk to the staff and they can tell me if Mike's boat is in or out. Look around and see if you can spot a Ram, will ya?"

A few minutes later, Tom waved his arms to signal Andrews to meet him on the far side of the marina. "I see a couple of Rams, Conner. They both have Good Year tires; and if I remember the photo you showed me a while back I identified Michelins."

"The dock manager says Mike drives a black Ram."

Tom pointed. "Well, I'll be. Look two rows down. You got the photo?"

Andrews opened a folder, withdrew the tire print and handed it to him. The imprinted Michelin trademark verified the make; and fresh tire tracks behind the Ram pickup provided more evidence.

Tom placed the photo close to the sand and nodding up and down exclaimed, "Look here, Conner, these indentations match perfectly to the ones in the photo. See there's even a small gouge in the edge of the tread where he may have run over something sharp. I say we'd better catch the judge before she calls it a day."

Andrews let out an enthusiastic, "Yes! This is the first real break we've had in the case. You ever get tired messin' with tires you might consider law enforcement, my friend."

"Nah -- a whole lot safer changin' tires. So, this guy's a suspect in that McNeil murder?"

"Can't say for sure why his truck was at the beach parking lot that night; but I need you to keep this information under your hat until the case is solved, okay?"

Tom was quick to respond, "What Ram? What tires? I didn't leave the shop all day. You've got my word on it." A handshake sealed the deal.

Chapter Nineteen

Melino was so excited when he heard Andrew's news that he had difficulty putting it out of his mind. A restless night, resulting in tousled bed sheets bore evidence that he hadn't slept much. For reasons he couldn't explain, he didn't feel tired but energized. *Finally, a solid lead!* By lunch, a molded cast of the truck tires would prove the Ram was at the parking lot on September 7.

Collins verified that the batteries Alana bought at the convenience store came from the D section of the display. Nick mulled this over as he dressed for work. Why did she need a flashlight at that hour of the morning?

At ten o'clock, Sheriff Kimbal stuck his head in the doorway of Nick's office and offered his support. "Hear you got a lead in the McNeil case. I know your team's had their nose to the grindstone on this one. It'll break soon. You're a real Pitbull, Nick. You never turn loose of something when you get a good grip on it!" He turned to go then swung back around. "Oh, I meant to tell you, sorry to hear about Penny. How's she doing?"

"She'll be fine. Thanks for asking. She's got a new appreciation for the MADD organization." Nick's complexion reddened. "So does her father; and it's been an enlightening experience if you get my drift."

" I do, Nick; and sometimes that's what it takes." The sheriff smiled as he gave Nick the thumbs up sign.

Whenever Nick had a tough case, he got out the reports and read them from the first line to the last over and over. His men's work was above reproach but there was always a chance that something could have slipped through the cracks. He was on a page titled 'Evidence Collected', when he stopped and quickly dialed Meyer's extension.

"Meyers, Nick. I need you to bring the McNeil articles collected at the beach to my office now, please."

"Yes, sir; I'm on it."

Ten minutes later, Meyers walked into the office and placed a sealed box on Nick's desk.

"We finger printed everything in here. The report should be in that folder."

Nick picked up the report and his eyes scanned the listed articles. No other finger prints except Lyndy's were listed beside each one. He wasn't surprised. But he needed to inspect a particular item in the box one more time.

"Hand me that box of gloves on the shelf, detective. I believe you'll see there's one piece of evidence here that got overlooked."

"Boss, I know everything in this box was checked for prints. Took it to the lab myself and watched the guy do it."

Nick pulled the top drawer of his desk open and picked up a pen knife. The tape on the box made a searing sound as the blade made a precise cut down the middle. Each article was individually labeled and sealed in a separate zippered plastic bag.

Meyers watched with intense curiosity. It wouldn't be the first time he saw Melino pull off something that no one else had given any thought to. Careful not to contaminate the objects, Nick picked through them until he found what he wanted. He pulled out the flashlight.

"Nick, the flashlight's been done. Lyndy's right hand prints are all over it."

"How 'bout the batteries?" A half-smile crossed the elder detective's face.

Meyers banged the palm of his hand against his forehead and his eyes grew wide. "Of course; the batteries! Why didn't I think of that? Alana bought flashlight size D batteries. You scored again, Boss."

"Just a hunch. I can be wrong but if the prints on the batteries do not match the ones on the flashlight cover, we may have hit pay dirt. Get this over to the lab and tell them their lives depend upon fast results."

"But," Meyers commented, " if they are different, we have nothing else to match them to other than running them through the data base."

"Oh, yes, we do! This ole dog has one more trick up his sleeve. Go." Nick handed Meyers the plastic bag and sat down with a sigh. If his hunch was right, it would be one of the saddest days of his life.

Chapter Twenty

A half-eaten sandwich lay on a napkin on Nick's desk. The uneasiness in his stomach was not from hunger pangs but nerves. *Who put the batteries in the flashlight?* His gut feeling told him the prints were the key to unlocking a mystery. His eyes kept returning to the phone as if willing the lab to call and release the tension he felt in every fiber of his body.

At last the moment arrived. The ringing phone shattered the stillness and startled Nick out of his thoughts.

"Melino."

"Hey, Nick, get ready for this." The lab tech continued, "The prints on the flashlight and the prints on the batteries do not match."

"Yes!" interrupted Nick. "That's the news I've been waiting to hear. Have Andrews run them through the usual channels and do me a big favor, will you, Sandra?"

"Sure, Nick, if I know you, you're on to something."

"I just may be; listen, I know it's almost quitting time but hang around and take one more set of prints for me."

"From the batteries?"

"No. I have to run home and get something. Won't take me long, promise."

"You're not going to tell me, are you?" she teased.

"Suspense is what we live on, isn't it?"

"Get outta here! The clock's ticking."

Closing in on a killer always sent the adrenaline in Nick's body soaring. It took all he had to keep from speeding as he maneuvered his way through traffic to Willow Lane. Once in his driveway, he jumped out of his car, leaving the door open and rushed toward the front entrance. Penny opened the door just in time to see her father rush past her and go into the kitchen.

"Hello to you, too. What's the hurry?"

"I'm looking for a brown paper bag. It was by the microwave. Did you move it?" Nick's eyes darted from one end of the counter to the other.

"It was in the way so I put it on the table. What's in it? Must be a big deal?"

"It could be,"offered Nick as he picked it up and started back outside. "I'll know shortly and then if you have dinner cooked by the time I return, I'll let you in on the mystery package. Deal?" He blew his daughter a kiss and the door slammed behind him.

Sandra, already gloved and ready to proceed, gave Nick a quizzical look as she tore the paper away from the object within. "A beer glass! From Southern Shores Seafood! That's a great place to get shrimp. Have you tried them?"

"I have. Many times. I'm a regular customer; that's how I got hold of this."

"So what's the connection with the battery prints?"

Nick's voice lost some of its enthusiasm and he looked at Sandra with sober eyes.

"If they match, I've found Lyndy McNeil's killer."

Normally, Nick left the print lifting to the lab techs and went on with his business but the urge to know the truth was too powerful and he stayed to watch the process.

Sandra looked at the glass to see if there were any obvious signs of prints and then asked Nick, "Who put the glass into the bag?"

"Alana, the owner's wife."

"Did you or anyone else handle it after you got it home?"

"It hasn't come out of the bag. My daughter moved it from the counter to the table but she never opened it."

"I'm guessing Alana picked it up by the top in order to place it into the bag so we'll start dusting from top to bottom. This black graphite ought to show her prints pretty well. Sometimes I use white dust; but it depends on the background."

Nick watched how carefully Sandra handled the vessel. Erasing a print or leaving a smudge with her gloves could complicate the whole process and destroy irreplaceable evidence.

"The less powder needed to bring up the print the better," she explained shaking any excess off the brush. "See? Lines and whorls are beginning to form. Looks like a thumb and a couple inches over I see a forefinger. Let me use the clear tape now to lift these and get them on a card."

"I admire your patience. If it was left to me, I'd have already blown it."

Sandra chuckled. "If I had to look down the nose of a Glock, or face some of the other things you see, Nick, my hands would be shaking like a leaf in a hurricane."

After filling in the proper documentation, she showed Nick the prints. "Perfect! They don't lift off any cleaner than that. And now, for the final verdict. Are they going to match the previous ones on the batteries?"

Nick's pulse raced and he took in short breaths while he watched Sandra's expression. Her lips pursed and as if verifying Nick's suspicions, she nodded her head while she looked into the magnifying glass.

"Come closer, Nick. You might want to see this for yourself. Notice how the lines are exactly the same on both thumb cards. They start out separated but as they get closer to the tip of the thumb, they almost merge. The prints from the batteries and the prints from the glass are identical. You've got sufficient evidence to make an arrest."

There was no elation in Nick's response. "You know Sandra, even when things go right, sometimes this job just plain stinks!"

Nick needed some time to clear his head in order to proceed in a professional manner. He called Andrews and filled him in on the latest developments.

"See if you can get Meyers and Collins in my office in an hour. We need to go over every detail and plan our next move. By this time tomorrow, as much as it pains me to do it, our number one suspect will be behind bars."

Chapter Twenty-one

Sharply at seven-thirty a.m. the following morning, two patrol cars fell in line with the early rush of traffic as drivers made their way to work. Andrews looked at Nick in the driver's seat. His back and shoulders were rigid and tanned fingers gripped the wheel so hard his knuckles turned white. Weary eyes looked neither left nor right but remained fixed on the cars in front. The muscles in his face tensed the closer they came to their destination. As the sign for Southern Shores Seafood came into view, he picked up the radio and gave a command.

"Meyers, Andrews and I will go in and make the arrest. One of you stay in the car but the other needs to go around back in case our suspect bolts."

"Read you, Boss."

Nick took a deep breath and parked the car near the entrance. Andrews picked up on Nick's feelings.

"You want me to take the lead? I sense this is a tough one for you."

"Thanks, partner, but I made a promise to Lyndy and as difficult as this arrest is going to be, it's my job. Let's go."

The sign in the window indicated that Alana was ready for business so Nick opened the door. The familiar dingle of the bell caught Alana's attention and she smiled when she saw Nick.

"Good morning; you're out shopping early. What can I get you today?"

"We're here on business, Ma'am," returned Andrews.

Nick gave the shop a quick survey before asking, "Alana, is Mike around?"

Alana's smile disappeared and she saw the serious side of Nick Melino. "Yeah. He's out back unloading last night's catch. I'll go get him."

As she turned to go, Andrews put his hands palm up and moved to block her way. "I'll get him; you stay here."

By now Alana's cheeks turned from a delicate pink to a pasty white. "What's going on, Nick?"

"Lock the front door and turn the window sign to closed."

She complied and within seconds, the sound of heavy boots on the concrete floor brought Mike face to face with Nick, Andrews at his side. "What the ...! What right do you have bustin' in here ordering us around?"

Nick wasted no time. "Alana Perkins, you are arrested on suspicion of murdering Lyndy McNeil."

Alana's knees grew weak and she stumbled against the fish display cooler. Before she had time to respond her husband shouted, "Now wait just a cotton-pickin' minute! That's the craziest thing I ever heard. She and Lyndy were best friends. Ain't that so, Hon?" Beads of sweat sprang out on Mike's forehead accentuating his anger. "And you of all people ought to know that, Melino!"

Mike placed his arm around his wife's shoulder as shock registered on her shaken face and tears streamed down ashen cheeks.

"Read her rights, Andrews."

Alana made no denial but looked at Mike with pleading eyes. "Call our lawyer. I'm not saying a word."

The click of the cuffs on Alana's wrists was more than Mike could handle. Between sobs he begged, "Tell me it isn't true Babe. It can't be true."

As Andrews led Alana out to the patrol car, Nick tried to console the distraught husband. "I'm as shocked as you, Mike, but we have the proof. Your lawyer can meet us at headquarters. I'll be interviewing Alana this afternoon. Can't tell you how long it will take. Depends on how co-operative she'll be. If you want to post bail, the judge on duty will hear the facts, and then render a decision. Let me tell you something else. We have a court order to make a cast of your Ram's tires. Believe me, I'm sorry. See you over there."

Andrews seated Alana in the back of the patrol car and then slipped in behind the wheel. For a second, Nick and Alana's eyes locked in silent confrontation as he peered through the back window. Her cold, resolute eyes showed no emotion but stared right through him. Nick felt a burning desire to verbally lash out at this woman who feigned friendship, but instead he turned away, climbed into the front seat and slammed the door shut. The drive to headquarters seemed like it took an eternity. He couldn't wait to get her booked and start the process of questioning her.

The radio crackled as he spoke to dispatch. "Jerry, Melino. Call Detention and tell them we have a female suspect in custody and we'll be delivering her to them shortly."

"Read you. I'm on it."

It didn't surprise Nick that Mike followed on their tail but the second he got out of his truck and ran up to the patrol car, Nick informed him he'd have to stay in the waiting room while his wife went through the booking process.

"What are they going to do?" he asked.

"She'll have to give personal information. Name, address, phone and social security number. Of course, she'll be fingerprinted and photographed. Then a staff nurse completes a medical examination."

Mike's voice trembled. "How do I get hold of the judge? I got to get her out of here, Nick. I've got money put away."

"Depends on how busy he is today. We have to present the facts as we know them and then it's up to him." Nick lay a hand on the anxious man's shoulder, "Considering the crime, Mike, the judge may deny bail. You need to know that."

#

The morning's tension left Nick craving his usual caffeine and he walked into the lounge and straight to the coffee machine. As he sipped his brew, it dawned on him that news of Alana's arrest was ripe fodder for the news media. Katherine McNeil and Heather deserved to hear this latest development from him -- not the local channel.

Who should I call first? Katherine or Heather? He walked back to his office and pulled out the file. Nick hesitated then made his decision. To hear that Alana, someone the family knew and trusted, was suspected of murdering Lyndy might trigger a heart attack in Katherine. *Better to call Heather.*

The Atlanta number rang three times. Nick drummed his fingers on his desk anxious to hear Heather's voice. Finally, a sweet southern drawl said, "He-l-lo."

"Heather, this is Lieutenant Melino. I have news for you. I suggest you sit down because what I'm going to tell you is shocking."

A gasp resonated through the line. "It's not Grandmother is it? Has something happened to her?"

"No, as far as I know your grandmother is fine." Nick heard a sigh of relief as he took a deep breath. "We made an arrest in your mother's case this morning."

Before he continued, Heather's anxious words cut him off. "Mom's murderer? Lieutenant who was he?"

"Our suspect isn't a male. A female has been charged."

"A woman! Good heavens! The only females in Gulfview Mom had any frequent contact with since she left were Grandmother and Alana. And they were best friends."

Melino let silence speak for itself.

It took but a second for Heather to get the message. Nick heard a sob on the other end of the line as he visualized the disbelief and shock Heather must have experienced.

"No! Oh, no! Not Alana. Mom trusted her," Heather protested. The sobbing turned into heart wrenching cries. "Why? Why did she kill my mother?"

"We haven't questioned her yet. She's still in the booking process so there's been no confession. Heather, the reporters are going to swarm all over this story, if they haven't already picked up the news of an arrest on their scanners. I don't want your grandmother hearing it second-hand. I wanted to give you the opportunity to speak to her first, but if you'd rather I go over. That's my job."

Nick sensed she was fighting for control. "Lieutenant, thank you for your consideration but Grandma needs me now. I live close to the airport and it's only a forty-five minute flight."

"May I make a suggestion?"

"Of course."

"Call me when your plane lands and I'll pick you up. It might be easier if I were present, too. If I know your grandmother she'll want all the details and the interrogation should be over by this afternoon."

"Thank you, Detective. Let me jot down your number and I'll see you later."

After an exchange of cell numbers, Nick concluded the conversation. "I know this has been bitter-sweet for you but soon you'll know the truth. Have a safe flight."

#

Heather closed her tear-filled eyes and murmured aloud, "I've got to get a grip." Her slender body trembled until it took all her willpower to overcome the weakness

148

and heaviness she felt pulling on her arms and legs. She took several deep breaths and finally her breathing calmed and her stomach nerves quit tingling. Never in a million years would she have imagined Alana wanted to harm her mother. *But why? Was there something between them Mom never told me about? No, there must be some mistake! The killer should have been some pervert who wandered the beach that night seeking his victims. Not mom's best friend!*

Like a burst dam, question after question flooded her mind demanding answers. Did this new revelation in the case exonerate her father? Gattett recently called Heather to say that he was leaving Gulfview and had accepted a coaching position with Florida State. She understood his need to put the past behind him and start afresh. They promised to keep in contact.

Grandma, I need to get to Grandma! Weak-kneed, Heather got to her feet and located her cell phone. After explaining to the ticket agent that there was a family emergency, she secured a reservation. In two hours, she'd be on a flight to Gulfview. A quick call to Katherine prepared her grandmother for her arrival. It was all Heather could do to keep from blurting out the astounding revelation of an arrest in her mother's murder but the timing wasn't right. She bent the truth and told her grandmother she was lonesome and wanted her company.

As Heather gathered belongings to pack, a knot in her stomach tightened. What dreadful details waited for her in Gulfview?

Chapter Twenty-two

It was after lunch before Judge Morris made his decision whether or not to grant bail for Alana.

After hearing the evidence against her, his answer was swift and blunt. "Your request for bail is denied. You shall remain in custody until a trial date is set. You have a right in this country to presume innocence until proven guilty but the matching fingerprints on the batteries and glass prevent me from granting you bail. The crime you're charged with took another's life. No one on this planet has the right to do that. You're dismissed to Officer Lang."

Nick stepped up to the deputy and said, "Officer, as soon as she's dressed out, bring her to room four. Her lawyer is here and we need to get on with the questioning."

Alana walked past her old friend, her face expressionless and devoid of emotion. She remained silent.

What's going on in that mind of hers? Will she confess or am I going to have to drag the truth out of her? Either way, this is one interrogation I could have never imagined I'd have to make.

Back in his office, Nick dialed Andrews and filled him in on the call he'd made to Heather.

"She texted me a few minutes ago that her plane lands at three. Yeah, I know, it's a tough assignment acting as chauffeur for a beautiful woman, but listen, someone has to do it. That's why I'm giving it to you."

"You're kidding?" Andrews said. "My lucky day!"

"Thought you'd be pleased. You do realize you owe me one, don't you?" teased Nick. "To be honest, I'm not sure how long this interview with Alana is going to take and I don't want to cut it short. It's already getting on to one o'clock. Call me when you're leaving the airport and if possible I'll meet you at the McNeil's."

Nick cleared his throat in a commanding manner. "Andrews, keep it professional; you're still on duty."

"You can count on me, partner." Nick heard, as his mind's eye pictured, a mischievous grin on Conner's face.

From past experiences, Nick knew interrogations did not always go as investigators intended. Good strategy was the difference between success or failure. *How was it best to approach Alana? It wasn't as though they were strangers. He knew her background—at least he thought he did until Martin confessed her parentage. That's an ace up my sleeve and I'll use it.* He concluded that a soft approach would work best. There was no advantage to be gained by using accusation at the beginning of the interview since her body language shrieked embarrassment and defiance.

Setting the stage to make sure all the physical logistics for an interrogation were in order was a trademark of Nick's professional career. He tolerated no distractions.

With Andrews on another mission, Nick dialed Collin's extension and made a request. "I need you to sit in on the McNeil interview and take notes. Check to be sure the video camera is ready to roll." Nick listened as Collins responded then continued, "Yes, bring a tape recorder. I like to have a back-up. See you in fifteen minutes. Thanks."

As Nick walked toward the interrogation room, he recognized Joe O'Hare, Alana's defense attorney. The two men shook hands. "We meet again, my friend. Come in and take a seat."

The room was small. Ten by ten, sparsely appointed with no windows, except for a two-way mirror. A small table and four wooden chairs were all that furnished the room. One chair remained at the table for the detective who operated the recording device and the other three were placed in the center of the room in strategic positions. Two chairs sat side by side; the one on the left was for attorneys and the one on the right was for suspects. The remaining one, reserved for the interrogation officer sat directly in front of the suspect. Nick learned long ago that having a physical barrier between him and a suspect presented a psychological barrier as well. It was better to eliminate such barriers, to plant the idea in the suspect's head that they were simply sitting down for a casual conversation.

Collins stuck his head in and asked, "Ready?"

Nick nodded. "Bring her in."

The bright orange jumpsuit Alana wore caught Nick's attention as soon as she entered the room. Gone were the casual capri's and tee-shirt. Her hair was drawn back in a ponytail and what little make-up she'd applied earlier that morning was smeared by trails of tears.

Nick motioned for Alana to take the seat in front of him. Having been in this room on other occasions, O'Hare needed no instruction but sat down next to his client.

Alana's downcast eyes lifted the second Nick started to speak. "Alana, do you understand the charges that have been made against you?"

She began to nod her head in agreement but Nick urged her on. "I need a verbal response, please."

Her strained voice answered in the affirmative.

"Alana I'm familiar with a good bit of your background but for the record, what was the relationship between you and Lyndy McNeil?"

"We grew up together. My mother was Robert McNeil's assistant. Lyndy was my best friend."

"She was more than a friend, wasn't she?"

"What do you mean?"

"Your half-brother spilled the beans. Told me about the affair between his father and your mother."

Anger flared and she muttered, "He promised never to tell anyone! Told me I might even be owed an inheritance after his mother dies."

"Martin McNeil is another issue. We're here to discuss you and Lyndy. After she moved away, how often did you see her?"

"Whenever she came home for visits--two maybe three times a year. I drove up to Atlanta a couple times. E-mail kept us in contact."

"Whose idea was it to organize a reunion?"

"Ours…I mean mine."

"Did Lyndy help?"

"She sent out the invitations and recorded the number coming."

"Sounds like you knew her pretty well." Nick shifted his body in order to look directly into her eyes before asking his next question. "The night of the reunion did Lyndy indicate to you that she was upset?"

Alana's fingers stroked the sides of the jumpsuit and her answer came quickly.

"No. Nothing."

"You saw no indication that she was planning to take her life?"

"You saw her Nick," the tone of her voice reeked of bitterness. "Laughing and joking with everyone. Even flirting with all of the men, as usual. But she still committed suicide. I can't believe it."

Nick watched as Alana's eyes flitted back and forth. They refused to focus on his face. He deliberately stared at a woman he believed was grasping at straws and let a moment of silence pass between them before asking, "Did she? Did she really commit suicide?"

Before Alana responded, her lawyer cut in. "You don't have to answer that."

Avoiding a direct response to Nick's question, Alana became defensive. "You told Martin and Katherine a gun was found by her side. I know she carried a gun. She told me a woman living alone needed protection."

"You're correct; her prints were on the gun."

A smug look of satisfaction settled on Alana's face.

Nick decided to put a little more pressure on his suspect and continued his questioning.

"What time did you leave the party?"

"About midnight. Lyndy and I cleaned up. She left and I wasn't long after."

"Where did you go?"

"Home."

"No stops?"

"None."

"Alana, we have the surveillance video from the In and Out convenience store."

Color rose in her cheeks as Nick proceeded. "Your Ram truck drove up around twelve ten and you went into the store."

She squirmed in the chair and offered an explanation. " Oh, that. Mike asked me to replace the batteries in a flashlight he kept in the truck. Guess I forgot."

"And you drove straight home?"

"Yes."

Nick pulled the photos of the Ram's tire prints from a folder and held one up to her.

"These prints taken at the beach parking lot match perfectly with your Ram's tires. Even down to the notch missing from the left tire." Everyone in the room sensed her change of attitude and saw her pink cheeks turn ashen.

"Now, I ask you again, where did you go when you left the convenience store?"

O'Hare chimed in and reminded Alana of her right to remain silent; but her attitude became combative.

"I told you." She waved her hand at the photos as if dismissing the evidence. "These don't prove anything."

"Then let me show you something that does. Again Nick opened his folder and removed more photos. Recognize these? The batteries you placed in the flashlight. Take a good look at the prints. Those are your prints; and you've already said that Mike asked you to replace the batteries in his flashlight- the same flashlight we found by Lyndy's body"

By now, Alana was biting her lips.

Nick continued, "Remember giving me this?" The photo clearly showed the glass with Southern Choice Seafood written on it. "These prints on it are identical to the prints on the batteries. You and I know the prints taken this morning will match both of these sets don't you?"

Alana turned to O'Hare and announced, "I want to speak to my lawyer- in private."

Both Meyers and Melino stood. "You have fifteen minutes," Nick stated as the door closed behind the two detectives.

A glance through the two-way mirror revealed a distraught client arguing with her lawyer. She paced the floor, sat down then got up again. Finally, she calmed down and began a serious conversation.

"She's on the hot seat and she knows it," Meyers commented. "What do you think she'll do?"

"Plea bargain's my guess. O'Hare knows we're holding all the aces."

The second the minute hand landed on the numeral three of Nick's watch, he opened the door, followed by Meyers.

Alana returned to her original chair. She bowed her head and wiped the falling tears from her cheeks.

O'Hare broke the silence. "She's willing to talk if you drop the first degree murder for a charge of manslaughter. You know only part of the story."

Nick despised this bargaining ploy. If a life was deliberately taken by another individual, he felt the murderer needed to be punished to the fullest extent of the law.

"I'll have to speak to the District Attorney's Office; I don't have the authority to make that call and you know that, Joe. This is going to take some time so take her back to detention, Meyers. Come with me, O'Hare."

A call to the District Attorney's office confirmed that he was able to meet with Melino and O'Hare. The two men walked in silence down a hallway to another wing in the building, each one mentally preparing their arguments.

Did I hear a slip-up on Alana's part when I asked who originated the idea of a reunion? Why did she say "ours" then quickly correct to say "mine". Was someone else involved? Who? Was she covering for them?

The answer from the prosecuting attorney in the District Attorney's office was swift. For a full confession including the names of any accomplices, the charge would be lessened to second degree manslaughter. Nick couldn't wait to hear the details the offer would produce from Alana. He reached in his jacket pocket for his cell phone.

"Bring her back. She's not finished." Melino increased his pace to the interview room. O'Hare came puffing up behind trying to keep up.

A few minutes passed before Alana confessed. "Lyndy had it all—wealth, beauty, charm. She was her daddy's little princess. Whatever Lyndy wanted; Lyndy got. Up until this past summer, I had no idea I had every right to claim him as my father, too."

Nick saw the jealousy and mounting torment in the tightened muscles around her mouth. He offered a comment. "This realization that you were never recognized as his daughter must have been painful."

"It still is. When I think back to the times he would slip a little extra money into my mother's paycheck and tell her to buy me something pretty or insist that I go with Lyndy to some vacation spot was just a ploy to ease his conscience. My mother was a fool! She let him use her." Alana trembled as past memories suddenly surfaced and she fought for self control.

"The atmosphere at the reunion opened all the old wounds, didn't it?"

Her voice was barely audible. "Martin suggested the reunion after the DNA proved we were kin. We both knew the reunion would bring Lyndy back to town. He told me that without her I'd be eligible for my part of an inheritance once Katherine died; and that it would be easy to fake Lyndy's suicide. I fell for it."

Nick recognized she was at a breaking point as more tears splashed against puffy cheeks and she drew up as if shielding herself from more pain.

"He's a man with an evil mind. He even told me, if his sister's death looked like suicide, it would give him a sympathy vote in the election for Senator."

Words continued to tumble from Alana's parched lips.

"Lyndy told me that after she left the Shifting Sands, she was meeting Garrett Williams by the old lifeguard platform down the beach a couple miles."

Nick's expression registered surprise. "You knew about that affair?"

"Friends share secrets - I've known for years who Heather's father was. I kept my word. Never told a soul."

"But you got to her first."

"She was waiting for him behind the dunes. They went there often. This time she got a surprise. I never said a word but simply shone the flashlight on my face. She never knew what hit her. Not a word was spoken between us. Jealousy, deceit revenge, call it what you want. Along with too much alcohol it all pushed me over the edge. You know they say there's a thin line between love and hate. I walked that line; but I crossed over it and shot her."

"Where did you get the gun? We traced it back to a gun shop but the owner claims it was stolen."

"Martin has connections. He took me out to the range and showed me how to use it." She raised her chin in pride. "I'm actually pretty good."

Collins started writing the confession statement while O'Hare shook his head. He knew his work as Alana's defense attorney was not going to be easy. The words kept pouring out of this tortured woman as though they'd been begging for the past four months to be set free.

"When I realized I had killed her, I followed Martin's instructions to make it look like a suicide. I rubbed sand on the gun to remove my prints then placed it in Lyndy's hand. I did the same with the flashlight. I thought it'd make sense that she'd need some kind of light in the dark.

That was a mistake; never should have left it there. Never thought about the batteries." She looked at Nick and almost smiled. "Pretty good, Nick. Guess that's why you're one of the best."

Nick ignored the compliment and continued the questioning. "Where's the necklace?"

Alana looked at him as if she misunderstood. "The necklace?"

Nick fought to suppress his irritation. "Don't play dumb at this stage, Alana. It won't help you in court because our deal will be off! Katherine and I are both witnesses to the fact Lyndy wore that gold necklace Robert gave her at graduation. She told her mother that evening she thought it fitting to wear it at the reunion. Skin tears on her neck showed that someone yanked it free. If I have to I'll get a search warrant."

"That necklace belonged to me as much as it did to her! My great grandmother owned it and Lyndy did nothing more to deserve it than I did. I have to live with the shame of being an illegitimate daughter. I believe I'm owed some compensation."

Nick continued the pressure. "Where is it?" No response. "It's your call, Alana. I can scuttle the deal we made with the District Attorney right now!"

Defeated, Alana got the message. "I don't have it. Martin told me he could take it to New Orleans and fence it for over twenty-thousand dollars." Alana's eyes blared with hate. "He said the proceeds would be my payment for a job well done. Lies! Nothing but lies! I gave it to him and haven't seen a penny since. My guess is he still has it."

"Do you have anything else to say, Alana?" Nick looked into the face of a hopeless woman, crushed, betrayed and abandoned by all she trusted.

Alana's voice broke and she hesitated with each word. "Tell… Katherine …I'm sorry. I …didn't mean…to hurt her. I never wanted to hurt Katherine. It was never about her."

Nick looked at Collins. "Ready for her signature?"

"One last line about the necklace," replied the detective as he completed the confession statement and then handed it to Nick.

"Wait a minute," O'Hare spoke up. "I assume you want me to read what's been written before you sign anything, Alana. Usual procedure, right Lieutenant?"

"Whatever your client decides, sir."

Alana accepted her attorney's advice and waited for his response. "No objections. The facts are clearly stated as witnessed by all in this room."

To be sure she understood the seriousness of signing a document that allegedly could put her behind bars for the rest of her life, Nick read every line to her.

Without hesitation, her trembling hand reached for the pen and scribbled her name.

A wash of sadness flooded over Nick and he wanted so much to cry out, "Why, Alana? Why? Did you hate her that much?" But he took a deep breath and calmly announced, "Collins, take her back to the detention officer." Without looking back, he picked up his folder and walked to his office.

Chapter Twenty-three

The revelation that Martin was Alana's alleged accomplice came as no surprise to Nick. But he had to prove it, and at this point, it was a 'he said-she said' situation. If Martin still had the necklace, it was a nail in his coffin. Usually when Nick was able to get a suspect to confess a crime and sign a statement he felt euphoric. Grueling hours and weeks of work didn't pay off this easily. But in this case, he felt his victory was bitter/sweet. True, resolution gave a sense of peace to the family but to know it was not a stranger who took Lyndy's life would always be hovering in the background, worse yet, if her brother proved to be the master-mind of the crime.

Nick struggled with his feelings on his way to his car. He started to open the door when another vehicle pulled up beside him and a Narcotics officer he recognized motioned for him to wait.

"Hey, Melino, got some news for you."

Nick's face brightened as he shook Johnson's hand. "Hope it's good."

"You still working on the McNeil case?"

"As a matter of fact, I got a confession this afternoon. Why?"

"Life is about to get a lot more interesting for you. I remember hearing you talk in the briefing room about a Brock Hamilton, a probable suspect, dropping out of sight."

Nick nodded. "All I can figure is that he got orders back to Afghanistan. He's a Marine, you know."

Johnson gave Melino one of those smiles that beg for more questions.

"Okay, what do you know that I don't?"

"A buddy of mine works narcotics in Biloxi. The guy was picked up for possession of heroin in September."

Nick's mouth dropped open and his mind raced. "I'm willing to bet my next paycheck it was the night of September seventh. So that's why he never showed up at the reunion."

"I can verify the date; no problem. Seems he's been smuggling the stuff from overseas on a military aircraft and selling it here in the States. An attentive pilot noticed that a survival kit onboard his airplane had been tampered with. When he opened it, he found the heroine. The brass called in the FBI and the rest is history."

Nick laughed and his sarcastic smirk left no doubt how he felt about Hamilton. "Oh, that's real smart now, isn't it? Looks like a good court marshal coming up. Fine with me; he deserves it!"

"Hamilton doesn't see it that way. Those Marines don't yell 'uncle' and he's determined to take no prisoners. Singing like a bird scratching for an easy deal. Says some well known figure here in Florida is in cahoots with him. Hamilton brings back the heroin and this guy uses it to pay off his gambling debts and other favors. The casinos then sell it to their high rollers. The FBI's had them on the radar for some time now; but it looks like Hamilton's co-operation will shut down that operation."

"So he hasn't named anyone yet?"

"My guess is he's holding out for a sweeter deal."

"I'll be talking to the FBI, too," Nick responded. "This murder investigation has taken a new twist and we may be looking for the same man."

"No kidding! You went to school with this Hamilton character, right? Must have known him well."

"It's a long story. Sometime I'll buy you a beer at Sandspur and give you the ugly details. Appreciate the news. There's a surprise around every corner with this job, isn't there? Thanks for brightening my day."

Johnson replied, "Wouldn't trade it for the world. Take care, Nick."

Once in his car, Nick took out his cell phone and dialed Andrews.

"Hey partner, hate to break up your visit; but I need you to meet me at the court house. Tell the ladies something's come up and we'll get back as soon as we can. Katherine hasn't been told Alana's in custody, has she?" Nick listened, and then continued.

"Good, hold off; this case may be bigger than we thought. I'll fill you in with some hot new details Narcotics just passed along. We're going to need a search warrant; so I'll go ahead and get things moving. See you in about thirty minutes."

#

165

The view from Martin McNeil's condo was breathtaking. Emerald-green water stretched as far as the eye could see until the Gulf blended into the puffy white clouds on the horizon. Martin paced in front of the expansive window oblivious to the scene before him. Sweat glistened on his worried brow and his mind refused to erase the words from a text message he'd received earlier.

McNeil, you're on borrowed time!

Martin knew he'd been on the casino's hit list ever since Hamilton messed up the September delivery. Not a day went by that he didn't look over his shoulder to see if he was being followed. He even checked under his car for some explosive device. His ex-brother-in-law could rot in jail as far as he was concerned. Getting stopped for speeding when you're concealing ten pounds of heroin was not smart; but then Brock was always heavy on brawn and light on brain.

Martin winced every time a knock came to the door. He figured it was only a matter of time before Brock made a deal with the FBI and fingered him as the king pin of the operation. Then there was Melino. How close was he to solving Lyndy's murder? Half-brother or not, Alana felt no allegiance to him, especially since he swindled her out of the necklace.

Feeling the squeeze of a predator, Martin's panicked emotions began to formulate escape options. Not only did he have a price on his head by the Biloxi mob but the state of Florida wanted his hide, too. As he pondered his situation, his gaze traveled across the Gulf. Mexico! He still had time to fly his Piper Cheyenne to Mexico. If nothing else, it would buy him some time. Besides, he knew the air route to Cancun like the back of his hand. How many beautiful women had he entertained at his favorite vacation spot over the years?

Martin took a swift survey of the spacious living room to see if there was anything he needed to pack and his eyes focused on a photo of his mother. She was the innocent victim in this family. Always had been. For years she catered to an unfaithful husband and gave her all to her children. *I'm sorry I let you down, Mom,* muttered Martin and he picked up the mother-of –pearl frame and brought the image of his mother to his lips.

Within twenty minutes, his bag was packed and sat by the door. Then he called the airport to prepare his plane for take-off. Before leaving, Martin opened a fake picture safe and took out a small package and slipped it into his jacket pocket. He had one more stop to make and then he was home free.

The private airport, located on the edge of town, housed several company planes as well as a distinctively painted one. Martin recognized the blue and white Seaworthy Boats logo on the tail of his craft as he drove over to the hangar. *Yes, it's fueled and on the tarmac. I'll be out of here in a matter of minutes. These guys are fast. Course Sandy and Joe have been servicing my plane for years. Don't recognize the new guy though. Must have hired more help. Business must be booming.*

Not wanting to linger, Martin made a hasty farewell to the men and climbed aboard. Twin turbines roared to life; and he breathed a sigh of relief. A feeling of freedom surged through his body as he prepared for take-off. Altitude and distance would separate him from his earthbound problems and he welcomed the panorama ahead.

Dad was smart when he bought this bird. She's fast and capable. Rivals the performance of a small jet at a fraction of the cost. Once I get this baby in the air, about two hours of flight time will bring me freedom and anonymity in a country where no one cares who I am, or where I come from, as long as I pay my way.

Smiling now, he taxied his Piper Cheyenne towards the runway. Future thoughts of selling the plane and using the money to live in luxury gave way to euphoria. Why, he might even turn over a new leaf and blend in with the locals, make a few connections with the 'powers that be', and relax while all this mess in the States blows over. Not once did he consider the fact that the boys in Biloxi never forget anything.

Martin turned his transponder to code 1200, made sure Com 1 was set to Local Traffic, and dialed in 123.10 for Panhandle Departure Control on Com 2. ATC had no idea he intended to leap into the blue and quickly slip away. Oh yeah, he knew he had to talk to them to make sure the military flight students zipping around the area didn't flip out when their windscreen suddenly filled with a two hundred and fifty knot Cheyenne clawing for altitude. Once clear of traffic, he intended to go radio-silent and become another one of dozens of unidentified blips on the radar screen, minding their own business on a beautiful cloudless day. Local controllers were used to talking to Zero November, and many of them knew the tail number belonged to Seaworthy Boats, hence its full call sign Sierra Bravo Zero November. The plane was reputed to frequently ferry upper crust folks to obscure destinations all over South America.

Robert's mantra, "Whatever it takes to sew up a sale," worked. Many a contract was finalized on this well-appointed ship, cruising at high altitude, with cocktails flowing.

Martin listened for a moment, and hearing no traffic on Unicom, he spoke into the microphone, "Cypress Point traffic, he called out again. Zero November is taking the active, straight out departure, runway one six. Moments later, with the nose of Zero November pointed down the centerline of the six thousand foot of blacktopped, well-manicured runway, he called, "Panhandle traffic, Seaworthy Zero November on the go runway one six, right turnout, south departure." Hearing no other aircraft that might challenge his right to take to the sky, he eased the throttles forward.

Powered by two screaming turbine engines, massive props clawed at the air and pressed Martin back into his leather bucket seat. "Wow, what a feeling!" he thought. He never ceased to be awed by the experience, and once again, this machine became part of his body and an extension of his personality - quick, flashy, and a force to be reckoned with.

A little hotter on the groundspeed than need be, he glanced about the horizon to make sure no overstressed, distracted military student pilot would be in his way, and eased back on the yoke. Zero November slipped skyward. Skimming over the sand dunes, and now zipping out over the emerald green waters of the Intercoastal Waterway, he eased into a gentle right turn and rapidly accelerated. There was no stopping him now. Retracting the gear, and still scanning for traffic, Martin reached over and switched to Com 2. "Panhandle Departure, Seaworthy Zero

November is a Cheyenne off Cypress Point southbound, VFR, code 1200."

"Seaworthy Zero November, this is Panhandle Departure. Good afternoon! Squawk code 1215 and say intentions."

"Departure, Zero November would like to go out thirty miles on this heading for a local test flight for about twenty minutes, and then return to Cypress Point."

Lying came naturally to Martin but departure control would never know it. He really planned to go out offshore, terminate the flight following service, descend below radar coverage, and push his Cheyenne as fast as it would go towards Mexico. He'd worry about Mexican air traffic control when he got there. In the meantime, he wanted to make sure he sped away before his flight attracted the attention of the Drug Enforcement Agency. He knew they operated a Cessna Citation Jet out of Pensacola and a P-3 Orion out of New Orleans; but, with this much lead, he also knew he could firewall his Cheyenne and be well out over international waters before either of them could take off and interfere with his plans. *Adios, America! Hola, Mexico!*

"Roger Zero November, radar contact three miles south of Cypress Point. Traffic at one o'clock two miles, a flight of two choppers, slow moving, eastbound. Mode C indicates 2,500. Say altitude."

"Zero November is passing one thousand eight hundred. Traffic in sight. I'll ease a little further to the right. Should pass well above and behind them. I'll throw a few more logs on the fire and go up to flight level one-eight-zero if that will help."

"Roger Zero November, clear that traffic and then climb to one zero thousand and standby! Break! Navy 212 and flight, is a twin Cheyenne at nine o'clock, one mile southbound, passing through two thousand seven hundred, has you in sight and will pass above and behind you."

"Departure, Navy 212, tallyho! No factor."

"Roger Navy 212, thanks. Break! Cheyenne Zero November, fly heading two one five, cleared to one six thousand, squawk 1110. Additional traffic is three o'clock, six miles, east southeast bound, an RJ, out of sixteen five climbing. As soon as you're clear of him, I'll have higher. Break! Trans Gulf 954, traffic is at your twelve o'clock, five miles, south southwest bound, a Cheyenne out of seven thousand for one six thousand."

"Roger Departure, Trans Gulf 954 has the traffic. We're passing seventeen three for flight level 310. Request direct Miami."

"Roger Trans Gulf 954, contact Center one three two point one five with your request. Good day!"

"One three two point one five, Trans Gulf 954 switching."

"Zero November copies. Cleared to one six thousand, turning to heading 215, squawking 1110. I have the RJ in sight."

"Damn, I'm good!" Martin told himself. "I should'a been an airline pilot. Never would've gotten into all this mess! I'll miss this place; but in a few more seconds, I'm outta here!"

"Okay Cheyenne Zero November, traffic is no longer a factor. Resume own navigation and you're cleared to flight level one eight zero. Stay with me and let me know when you're ready to head back to Cypress Point."

Seconds passed with complete silence. Sam Edwards, a seasoned air traffic controller of seventeen years took his position at the boards and began to familiarize himself with the day's traffic flow. He loved his job. And he loved working this traffic sector. "Busy enough to keep your adrenaline flowing," he mused, "but light enough to keep the heart beat under control." He'd often compared his job to a giant video game that you played for keeps. "Never a dull moment," he thought, waiting for Zero November's response.

"Zero November, Departure, did you copy clearance? Zero November, Panhandle Departure, come up one two three point one zero.

"Okay, idiot," Sam thought out loud. "Pay attention. We've got work to do here! Zero November, Departure!"

A chill swept through Sam's body. "This ain't right," he said, spinning left in his swivel chair and motioning for his supervisor to come over. He'd seen Zero November's transponder target change, indicating that it had been turned off, or failed somehow. And he knew that, even without a transponder, he should be seeing a raw radar return on Martin's airplane. But he wasn't. Switching up to one two one point five, the international VHF emergency frequency, he keyed his mike again.

"Cheyenne Zero November, Panhandle Departure on VHF Guard, radar contact lost fourteen miles south of Cypress Point. Reset transponder, squawk code 1110."

Two seconds later, a familiar voice broke the silence, as Sam looked up at the lights that indicated which frequency was in use. "Zero November," he thought, "'bout time, stupid! Do you think I want to play with you?" But it wasn't Zero November calling.

"Panhandle Departure, this is Trans Gulf 954 back with you. Hey listen. That Cheyenne you pointed out to us. We still see him; but he's headed straight down trailing flames. He's at our eight o'clock, about two miles. Do you need a fix on him?"

Stunned, Sam's jaw dropped as Trans Gulf954 called again, "Departure, he just hit the water! The Cheyenne hit the water! Looks like he's about five miles north of a cluster of oil platforms. What do you want us to do, Departure?"

Sam's 'giant video game' had suddenly pushed all of the weight of the world down on his shoulders. He knew he couldn't hit a 'pause' button to get out from under this one. This was real! And he had a plane down! This was one of the worse things that could happen to a controller because he still had to stay as cool as possible and focus all of his attention on controlling the other aircraft in his sector, even as his hastily assigned relief watched over his shoulder and waited for an appropriate moment to take over. Sam's supervisor was busily pushing buttons on the overhead console, notifying adjacent control facilities of an emergency in progress and reporting the details of this emergency to the Coast Guard Search and Rescue.

Mustering all of the cool that can only come with years of training and experience, Sam acknowledged Trans Gulf's information. "Thank you, Trans Gulf 954. Sorry you had to see that. Help is on the way. Trans Gulf954 return to Center frequency, please."

"Trans Gulf 954, roger, switching."

And then the questions began. Did Sam not see another target on the radar that might have collided with Zero November? Did he miss a call or some other indication that a tragedy was about to unfold?

News of the disastrous flight spread like wild fire around the town's small airport once Sam called the head of operations to determine how many people were onboard. Shock and unbelief was on everyone's lips. Except for the new man on the job; he knew why Martin McNeil and his Cheyenne met a watery death. He planted the bomb in Zero November's tail and set its barometric trigger to go off at 10,000 feet. Mission accomplished. Unnoticed, he sped away from Cypress Point Airport, en route to Biloxi to collect his reward. Business was "booming", indeed.

Chapter Twenty-four

At four o'clock, with search warrant in hand, Melino and Andrews knocked on Martin McNeil's condo door. No response. Several more attempts brought the same result.

"You lookin' for Mr. McNeil?" a voice came from around the corner of the building.

Melino turned and saw a young boy bouncing a basketball. "Yes, son, have you seen him?"

"He ain't here. Left a couple hours ago."

"Was he alone?" asked Andrews.

"Yep. Had him a traveling bag. Guess he's gone on vacation. He goes away a lot. I know 'cause I live next door."

Before the boy continued, Melino's cell phone interrupted. A quick glance indicated to Nick it was Sheriff Kimbal.

Andrews saw his partner's jaw drop and his conversation took on a serious tone.

"We're on our way; hope we get there before the media swarms in. I'll report to you later."

Andrews raised his eyebrows and gave Nick a quizzical look but asked no questions until they were in the car. "What was that all about?"

"You're not going to believe it. The kid may have been half right about McNeil, but this is one vacation that's permanent. His plane went down in the Gulf less than an hour ago."

Stunned, Andrews mouth popped open and it took a second for Nick's words to register. "What happened?"

"Sheriff doesn't have many details. The Coast Guard identified the plane from the Seaworthy Boats logo on the tail section that broke off. According to the company, Martin was the only one since Robert's death to fly that plane. We don't want Katherine and Heather hearing this on the six o'clock news. Step on it."

Despite the welcoming heat from the blazing pine logs crackling and popping in the stone fireplace in the McNeil mansion, Andrews sensed a chilling change in the atmosphere the moment Heather opened the door. What had happened in the short time since he'd left? Heather's face was ashen and mascara smudged her upper cheekbone as if she'd wiped tears away. She looked at both men and they saw relief in her eyes as she said, "Thank goodness you're here. Something strange happened shortly after you left, Sergeant Andrews. Come into the living room; Grandmother has something to show you."

Katherine sat in her winged chair looking pale and distraught. In her hand, she clung to a gold and emerald necklace. Nick recognized it at once. He walked over and bent down to get eye to eye with this wounded woman.

"It's Lyndy's, Lieutenant. Can you believe it?"

Nick studied the glittering gem stones and nodded his head in agreement. "But how did you get it?"

Katherine looked at Heather and asked, "Would you tell them the story, dear? I'm afraid I'm still in shock."

Without hesitation, Heather began, "The doorbell rang and a courier service handed me a package and asked me to sign for it. It was addressed to Katherine McNeil. No return address. I gave it to Grandmother and when she opened it, I thought she was going to faint. The necklace was laying in the bottom of a small box."

"Was there a note?" asked Conner.

"Nothing."

"Do you still have the box and the wrapping?"

"Yes."

Nick gave an explanation. "There may be prints."

A new light came into Katherine's eyes as she understood Andrew's purpose for asking. "Of course; prints could lead to Lyndy's killer."

Nick took a deep breath, and motioned for Heather to come closer. What he had to say was not going to be easy and he wanted Katherine to be supported by a member of her family.

"Mrs. McNeil, I called Heather and asked her to come and be with you because I have some disturbing news. Lyndy's killer signed a confession today."

A gasp escaped from deep within Katherine's throat and one word formed on her lips. Who?"

Heather reached for her grandmother's hand as Nick stumbled, "A-A-lana."

177

Katherine's shoulders shook first and like an avalanche, the trembling followed the length of her body. She buried her face in Heather's chest and it was several minutes before her strength and composure returned.

"Grandma, are you alright? Do I need to call Dr. James?"

"No, no. Just give me a minute to get my breath."

Everyone sat in silence as Katherine regained control of her emotions. Nick sensed the effort it took for Katherine to steel her strength for what was yet to come. Finally, she whispered, "Why? Tell me why?"

Nick's voice was gentle when he asked, "Mrs. McNeil, did you know your husband had another daughter?"

Katherine's voice strengthened, "I knew he'd been unfaithful. In fact, I challenged him about it and he admitted there had been another woman but there was no mention of a child. He refused to give me her name." Katherine took a lace hankie from her sleeve and dabbed her eyes. "I threatened to take Martin and Lyndy and go back to Texas so he promised it would never happen again. Lyndy meant everything to him; he couldn't bear to lose her."

As the truth dawned on Katherine, she put the pieces together on her own. "Alana's mother worked for Robert as his assistant. So she was the other woman." A long sigh followed. "How could I have been so blind? But I don't understand, did Alana know from childhood who her father was?"

"No. She found out only six months ago."

"Who told her?"

Nick hesitated but he knew this woman deserved to know the truth no matter how much it hurt. "Martin was suspicious about her parentage and talked Alana into getting a DNA test done. The results were positive. Alana felt cheated; especially when she saw Lyndy's privileged lifestyle. Since Robert and her mother were both dead, she took her anger out on Lyndy."

As Katherine listened, the matriarch of the McNeil home gained control. "Lieutenant, in effect you are telling me that had Martin not persuaded his half-sister to have the DNA test, Alana would never have known; and therefore my daughter's life would have been spared."

Both detectives nodded and agreed the crime was motivated by greed and jealousy.

Katherine turned to Heather. "Sweetheart, I'll need you to take me to visit my attorney, tomorrow. Your Uncle Martin will find out upon my death and the reading of my will that lightening does strike twice."

Andrews looked at Nick and knew his partner was about to deliver another blow.

"That won't be necessary, Heather."

Taken back, Katherine challenged Nick. "Excuse me, Lieutenant but this is a private family decision."

"Forgive me, Ma'am, but there's more to tell you. Martin's plane went down in the Gulf this afternoon. The Coast Guard is searching for his body as we speak. I'm so sorry."

This time, both women let out a shriek! They reached for each other and sobbed together. With eyes lowered and lips sealed, Nick and Conner sat quietly and let the women's emotions run their due course. Finally, with ragged breathing, Katherine uttered, "There are so many questions but I haven't the strength to ask them now."

"I understand," said Nick. When you're ready, feel free to come to my office and if you want to hear Alana's taped confession, I can make it available. An investigation will be done on Martin's death by the FAA. I guarantee it will be thorough and you'll get answers to your questions."

Andrews spoke up. "Is there anyone you'd like us to call?"

A look of love came over Katherine's face and she squeezed Heather's shoulders. "Not really; the only one left that means anything to me is sitting right here. We come from strong stock, Sergeant and we'll get through this too."

Heather smiled back at her grandmother and announced, "I was offered a position over at the University of West Florida teaching art appreciation so I'll be leaving Atlanta to live with Grandma."

Nick thought he saw a spark of life in Katherine's tired eyes as she commented, "It'll be like having Lyndy home again."

Taking a cue to leave, both men offered their sympathy and prepared to depart. Katherine insisted on seeing Nick to the door as Conner lingered a moment to speak to Heather. For an instant, as Nick watched the younger couple enter the foyer, his mind raced back in time and he felt his heart beat quickened. It was Lyndy's nuances all over again -- the flip of her head, the winsome smile and the confident stride. *Conner, my friend, you don't stand a chance.*

As the two men walked down the porch steps, Conner looked at his watch and made a suggestion, "Hey, we're off the clock; let's wrap this case up over a round at the Sandspur."

Any other time Nick would have jumped at the chance but not today. It was time to take a stand in his own life.

"Conner," he stopped and looked at his partner with a determination that startled Andrews. "I'm starting my New Year's resolution early this year. More time with Penny and less with a Bud. And let me give you a piece of advice. From what I hear, you need to spend less time at the Sandspur and more time studying up on Picasso and Rembrandt." Nick gave his partner a teasing smile. "Never know what a course in fine art can lead too."

The End

Made in the USA
Charleston, SC
06 August 2012